Country Roads
~ of ~
VERMONT

*A Guide Book
from Country Roads Press*

Country Roads
~ of ~
VERMONT

Molly K. Walsh
and
Joseph W. Cutts

Illustrated by
Dawn L. Nelson

Country Roads Press
CASTINE · MAINE

Country Roads of Vermont

Published by Country Roads Press
P.O. Box 286, Lower Main Street
Castine, Maine 04421

Text and cover design by Edith Allard.
Illustrations by Dawn L. Nelson.
Cover illustration by Gloria Clark.
Library of Congress Catalog Card No. 93-070216.
ISBN 1-56626-021-3

Printed in the United States of America.
10   9   8   7   6   5   4   3   2   1

To Baby A and Baby B, whoever you are

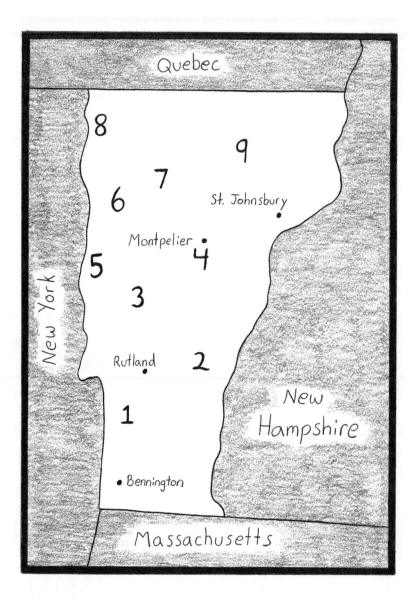

Contents

(& Key to Vermont Country Roads)

Introduction

Vermont, named after the French words for green mountains, is as lush and peaceful a place as any country traveler could hope to find.

In an age when sameness has mushroomed across the nation in strip developments, shopping malls, and franchise food outlets, Vermont remains distinctly individual, unto itself.

Vermont makes a striking portrait, each feature contributing to a face like no other. The rocky hill farms, cliff-sided lakes and sweet-scented apple blossoms; the muddy pastures, tumbledown barns and lollygagging cows; the soft-sloping mountains; the dark, dripping sap and the no-nonsense people—these are the images that linger.

Because the fourteenth state is so distinctive, visitors often refer to it as the land that time forgot, or never-never land. While Vermonters hotly debate the level of development in the state—and many feel it should not advance—Vermont is an unspoiled paradise compared to much of the United States.

The entire state population is under 600,000—less than many cities. Traffic on Vermont's two interstates is a trickle compared to that of an urban superhighway. Crowds are few, and quiet is abundant, despite the fact that the state is within weekend commuting distance of Montreal, Boston, and Hartford.

Country roads are the norm and rural landscapes are abundant. Keep in mind that Vermont is a small state:

Motorists can drive its length in just under five hours and its width in two or so. But don't let Vermont's small palm fool you. It is lined with a rich history, diverse terrain, and view after view of pastoral peace. It is no wonder Vermonters have a strong sense of place.

The routes outlined in this book are mostly suitable for all four seasons, though a sturdy vehicle is advised for winter and early spring exploration.

Before starting out, pick up an official state map for detail on Vermont's 14,000 miles of highway and roads. We've provided specific directions but the map will fill in the picture.

To simplify road designations, we've used the following abbreviations: I = Interstate; US = U.S. Route or Highway; State = State Route or Highway.

Visitors may also want to write ahead for a copy of the annual *Vermont Traveler's Guidebook*, which lists inns, restaurants, events, and county chambers of commerce. To order, write the Vermont Travel Division, 134 State Street, Montpelier, 05602. 802-828-3236.

Happy trails.

1 ~

Brandon to Bennington

From Burlington take US 7 forty-five miles south to Brandon. This trip begins in Brandon and ends in Bennington.

Highlights: *Antiques, pastoral views, charming inns, marble industry history; New England Maple Museum, Wilson Castle, Vermont State Craft Center, American Museum of Fly Fishing; home of Robert Todd Lincoln, Norman Rockwell country, Robert Frost's home and burial site.*

The Route

Head south from Brandon on US 7 to Pittsford, then take State 3 to Proctor and Proctor Road to Rutland. In Rutland, take US 7 to State 7A in Manchester. Stay on 7A through Manchester village, Arlington, and all the way to Bennington. The trip is eighty miles and will take at least 2 1/2 hours without stops.

This trek through southern Vermont is fairly well traveled, and for good reason. Aside from the natural attractions of lush farms and proud mountains, there are many historic sites and quaint towns to explore. Proctor boasts one of the only marble bridges in the world. Arlington, former home of Norman Rockwell, honors the artist with a museum, in which his former models work as guides. In Old Bennington, fans of Robert Frost make regular visits to his grave at the Old First Church.

Antique and gift shops line US 7, and many a weary traveler has found satisfaction at the cozy inns along the way. This drive isn't a long one, but there are more than enough stops to make it a daylong outing.

Entering Brandon from the north, the town's first greeting is a sign announcing that Stephen A. Douglas, "the little giant" who opposed Abraham Lincoln in the famous debates of 1858, was born here. The town's 4,000 residents are fastidious: The nineteenth-century Victorian and French Second Empire-style homes are in good repair, reminders of the town's prosperous industrial past, when local fortunes were made in marble, iron, and the manufacture of stoves, scales, and paint. Today, the town greens are clean and quaint, and the commercial row is tidy.

Parking is plentiful, in case you are tempted by one of the shops, restaurants, or bakeries in the town center. Quilters might enjoy a browse through the Vermont Made Furniture Outlet on US 7. It sells quilts, beds, duck decoys, and other competitively priced country homewares. If you're on the prowl for antiques, continue through town past the Civil War monument and veer left onto Park Street.

Nutting House Antiques specializes in early American furniture and unusual architectural elements, such as columns, capitals, pediments, and windows. David Laubscher, who owns the shop with his wife, Pam, is a garrulous type who prides himself on his historically accurate repairs and refinishing. He uses and sells buttermilk paints, which are still made according to the old recipe by the Sturbridge Paint Company.

2

A few doors down on Park Street, the Brandon Antiques Shop sells early furnishings and folk art paintings.

Whether or not you need lodging, it's worth stopping in at the elegant Brandon Inn on US 7 back in the center of town. The green-and-white awning greets visitors from all over the country who come to sit by the huge old fireplace, admire the gilt-framed beveled mirrors, and generally soak up the colonial ambience of this 1786 inn, which is listed on the National Register of Historic Places. It's open year-round.

Take US 7 out of town and into the open country. Rocky pastures, teetering silos, and old farmhouses create a vintage scene. The occasional elm soars against the Vermont sky, and sumac grows close to the road beside the barbed-wire and rail fences that line adjacent pastures.

About eight miles south of Brandon, just north of Pittsford, watch for a right turn indicating the truck route to Florence. This road leads to the first of four covered bridges in tiny Pittsford, starting with the 139-foot Hammond Covered Bridge, which is open to pedestrians but not cars. The Hammond Bridge was built in 1842 by Asa Nourse. It served the town faithfully until the Great Flood of 1927, when it floated off its abutments and ended up in a field a mile downstream. The bridge was hauled back to its place a few months later.

Each of Pittsford's four covered bridges is marked by a symbol on the Vermont state map. To see them, after the Hammond Bridge cross the railroad tracks and take your first left, continuing left when the road forks. Then take your next left back toward Pittsford and past the second bridge. Back on US 7, consider a stop at the New England Maple Museum. In addition to gifts, syrup, and maple candy—so sweet that even the most dedicated sweet tooths may be overwhelmed—the museum offers an exhibit about the history of sugaring in Vermont. Remember that it takes forty gallons of sap to yield just one gallon of maple syrup. The sap collecting and cooking

A typical covered bridge

process, the mysteries of the maple tree, and even sap-bucket making are illustrated at the museum.

From the museum, backtrack a few hundred feet north and take a left toward Proctor, passing two more covered bridges on the way, the Cooley Bridge and the Goreham Bridge.

It's just a few miles to Proctor, one of the most curious towns in Vermont. The marble sidewalks, marble buildings, and beautiful old marble bridge into town—one of the few in the world—are a testament to the 209-year-old marble industry in Proctor. Marble quarried in Proctor and nearby Danby was used in the Lincoln Memorial, the U.S. Supreme Court building, and many other grand buildings in and outside the country.

The Vermont Marble Company was founded in 1870 by Redfield Proctor and became the nation's primary source for marble statuary in the late nineteenth century. Immigrant workers, many of them Swedish, populated the company town, where the store, hospital, and houses were owned by Vermont Marble.

Three generations of Proctors would serve as governors of Vermont, and for many years marble was Vermont's top industry. Today the quarries are mostly inactive and after a long, slow decline, Vermont Marble announced in January 1993 that it would close. However, the museum and gift shop remain open. It is located in the heart of town and is visited by thousands of tourists every year.

The museum features replicas of the *Pietà* and the *Last Supper*, geological samples, a sculptor in residence, historic slides, and a factory viewing site where visitors can watch rough marble being polished and cut.

The gift shop sells marble vases, tabletops, sculptures, bookends, cutting boards, jewelry, and more, but the best bargains are found in a marble yard in front of the building. Here unpolished slabs and "seconds" of polished marble are sold by the square foot. There are slabs and chunks of all sizes, in both green and white.

From the Vermont Marble Company, follow the signs to the Wilson Castle, a lovely four-mile drive out of town toward our next destination, Rutland. On the way to the castle on West Proctor Road, the road runs along a curving river that is lined with trees. The muddy pasture is full of cows that gather and wait patiently at their gates when it's milking or feeding time.

The nineteenth-century brick castle appears around a bend, on the right at the top of a rise. With its turrets, domes, slate roof, and arched porches, it is an impressive edifice. The main house is in good repair, as are outbuildings across the road that now house a radio station, but one of the brick barns has caved in, looking wild and abandoned. Tours of the castle are available daily from mid-May to late October.

From the castle, continue south on Proctor Road, which connects to US 4, where you should turn left. Note J. P. Gawett and Sons, another marble and granite shop with bargain slabs in a yard out front.

If you're hungry, Flory's Snack Bar on the left will feed you in a hurry with hamburgers, hot dogs, and shakes year-round. Otherwise, forge ahead to Rutland, the second largest city in Vermont, with a population of 18,436.

The fine Victorian homes and marble-fronted buildings on Merchants Row in Rutland date back to the "Marble City's" heyday as a railroad center for outbound trains loaded with area marble. Today the economy is diversified with a variety of industries, including tourism. Many skiers pass through on their way to nearby Killington and Pico, occasionally stoking up at Rutland's many restaurants. We like the Sirloin Saloon for good cuts of beef and fish and an endless salad bar.

After rambling around Rutland, make your way back to US 7, and head south. Our next destination is Manchester, twenty-nine miles south. The suburban clutter of malls and such on the south end of Rutland quickly dissolves into green landscapes.

In Wallingford, eight miles south of Rutland, the Victorian Inn offers a tasty Sunday brunch. Afterwards, take some time to browse through the Wallingford Antiques Center and other inviting shops. You'll pass a charming old country cemetery full of hydrangeas, and then south of town you will come upon the White Rock Inn, a supremely restful-looking country bed and breakfast.

Continuing south, the road is lined with shops selling antiques, cheese, syrup, and Vermont crafts. Don't let the shops distract you, though, from the view of the Green

Mountain National Forest to the east and the Taconic Range of the Green Mountains to the west.

This drive is lovely year-round. In summer it is rich green, in fall colorful rust, amber, and yellow, and in winter the bare trees rise starkly against the blue-gray steeps. Ice formations collect where water will run come spring.

Nearing Manchester, you'll see the sign for State 7A. Follow it and head into one of Vermont's most visited towns.

The abundant chalets, inns, and restaurants cater to skiers who come to schuss Stratton and Bromley, fishermen who ply for trout in the Batten Kill, and another breed of hearty sportspeople: shoppers.

Manchester is crowded with dozens of outlet shops that draw bargain hunters from all over New England. Ralph Lauren, J. Crew, Benetton, Calvin Klein, Izod, Timberland, and Cole-Haan are just a few of the many labels represented here.

The mushrooming of outlet stores has left some old-time Manchester residents a bit disgruntled, in spite of the boost to the local economy. So thick are the tourists on some Saturday afternoons that locals have dubbed the main intersection of town "malfunction junction."

Rest assured, however, that by city standards the traffic here is quite tolerable. And despite the influx of tourists and outlets, Manchester has plenty of charm. Shop your way through Manchester Center, stopping for a literary respite at the Northshire Bookstore, one of southern Vermont's finest. Then walk or drive south on State 7A into historic Manchester village, a nineteenth-century summer resort that is still grand.

Marble sidewalks, mansions with sweeping porticos, and historic inns line the streets. The Equinox, named for the 3,825-foot mountain to the west of the village, is one of the oldest and poshest inns in town. Recently renovated, the white-pillared inn offers fine dining, a health spa, golfing, and expansive common areas. Other charming inns are nearby.

There are many attractions in Manchester village. If you aren't shopped out, visit the Vermont State Craft Center, and browse through Vermont-made crafts, art, and furniture.

Or pop into the Johnny Appleseed Bookshop, which from 1935 to 1965 was run by poet Walter Hard and his novelist wife, Margaret. Today it has an extensive collection of used books, including many rare titles.

Hildene, the former home of Robert Todd Lincoln, son of Abraham Lincoln, is also a popular destination. In summer (mid-May through October), the twenty-four-room Georgian manor and its elaborate gardens are open daily for tours. Concerts, festivals, and polo matches are staged on the 412-acre grounds. In winter, the snowy estate is tracked with cross-country ski trails accessible for a modest fee.

Lincoln first visited Manchester with his mother, Mary, shortly before his father was assassinated. Many years later he built Hildene, where he would die in 1926. Lincoln family members occupied Hildene until 1975.

For fly-fishing aficionados, Manchester is a delightful stop. Not only is it adjacent to one of Vermont's best-known trout streams, the Batten Kill, it is also the headquarters of Orvis, the venerable fly-fishing and outdoor outfitter.

Orvis sells and rents equipment, in addition to teaching fly-fishing courses. True fly-fishing buffs might also want to visit the American Museum of Fly Fishing on Seminary Avenue, where you can admire Ernest Hemingway's old pole.

For stunning views in the warm months, cruise up Sky Line Drive, a five-mile toll road that climbs Mount Equinox to the Skyline Inn. The road is open from May to October.

After an invigorating hike or drive, visit one of Manchester's many gourmet restaurants. The Black Swan is highly recommended, though pricey. Less expensive options are also available.

From Manchester, continue south on State 7A, watching in summer for a spectacular field of sunflowers on the right, just out of town.

As you head toward Arlington, cornfields and cow pastures replace the grand architecture of Manchester village. Shops appear here and there, selling everything from baskets to stained glass.

Arlington, an old-fashioned New England town, is famous in Vermont as the home of illustrator Norman Rockwell from 1939 to 1953. Its small-town Yankee values inspired some of Rockwell's most famous work, including the *Four Freedoms* series and *The Gossips*, both of which feature local people.

Rockwell coaxed dozens of his neighbors into posing for him, as the models-turned-guides will tell you at the Norman Rockwell Exhibition and Gift Shop in the center of town. Though cluttered, it's a friendly place. It's delightful to meet the volunteer guides and see them as they were forty and fifty years ago in a Rockwell illustration. Marjorie Brush, a guide who modeled with her family for *The Country Doctor*, remembers Rockwell as a charming fellow who would often coach his models into displaying just the expression he wanted for an illustration. The models will even give you directions to Rockwell's old house, now open to guests as the Inn on the Covered Bridge Green. The five-room, $125-a-night inn is open year-round.

From Arlington, head south, through what is known as the Valley of Vermont, into Shaftsbury and on toward Bennington. Sleepy Shaftsbury is notable mainly as the former home of poet Robert Frost. The current occupant of Frost's home is none other than Norman Lear, TV producer of "All in the Family" fame.

The quick trip to Bennington offers more rolling country and farmland. The occasional prissy antique shop is likely to share the roadside with a John Deere farm equipment dealership. Follow the signs into downtown Bennington and watch for the first view of the Bennington Battle Monument, a striking, 306-foot granite obelisk that was erected in 1891.

Heading into Bennington, note the Blue Ben Diner, a favorite hangout for students from Bennington College and nearby Williams College south across the Massachusetts border. Downtown, there are shops, restaurants, and some historic buildings. In the 1800s, Bennington was home to paper mills, potteries, gristmills, and a firebrick factory.

Manufacturing is the modern economic mainstay in Bennington, population 17,000, although it is also known as a college town. Bennington College, one of the most expensive private colleges in America, is a creative well for artists, dancers, and writers. Its campus, with a mix of classic New England buildings and 1960s construction, is a short drive from downtown.

Perhaps the best of Bennington is Old Bennington, the historic hilltop section of town, which harbors one of the greatest concentrations of Georgian and Federal structures in the state. It was near Old Bennington that, in 1777, a band of Green Mountain Boys under Seth Warner helped to defeat the troops of British General John Burgoyne in a pivotal battle that boosted Yankee morale.

To get to Old Bennington go west uphill on Main Street, or State 9. One of the first attractions is the stone and pillared Bennington Museum on the left. In front, two lifelike dalmatian statues guard the door. Inside, the museum's many treasures include memorabilia from the Battle of Bennington, the oldest revolutionary flag in existence, a collection of historic local ceramics, and the largest public collection of paintings by beloved folk artist Anna "Grandma" Moses. The Bennington Museum is open daily all year.

From the museum continue up the hill, turning right on Monument Avenue past a row of exquisite historic homes, heading toward the Bennington Battle Monument. Night or day, winter or summer, the monument is spectacular. An elevator takes visitors up to an observation point high in the monument from April 1 to November 1.

Enjoy the view and then proceed back down Monument Avenue to the Old First Church, which was built in 1805. In addition to its architectural significance, the church has become a shrine of sorts, for it is here that Robert Frost is buried. Many people stop by to remember the poet, following signs to his grave, and perhaps musing on the last stanza of Frost's 1942 poem "The Lesson for Today":

> I hold your doctrine of Memento Mori.
> And were an epitaph to be my story
> I'd have a short one ready for my own.
> I would have written of me on my stone:
> I had a lover's quarrel with the world.

In the Area

All phone numbers are in area code 802.

Vermont Made Furniture Outlet, Brandon, 247-0117

Nutting House Antiques, Brandon, 247-3302

Brandon Antiques Shop, Brandon, 247-3026

Brandon Inn, Village Green, Brandon, 247-5766

New England Maple Museum, Pittsford, 483-9414

Wilson Castle, Rutland Center, 773-3284

Vermont Marble Exhibit, Proctor, 459-3311 ext. 436

The Inn on the Covered Bridge Green, Arlington, 375-9489

Sirloin Saloon, Rutland, 773-7900

Victorian Inn, Wallingford, 446-2099

Wallingford Antiques Center, 446-2450

White Rock Inn, Wallingford, 446-2077

Northshire Bookstore, Manchester, 362-2200

The Equinox, Manchester Village, 362-4700

Johnny Appleseed Bookshop, Manchester Village, 362-2458

Black Swan Restaurant, Manchester, 362-3807

Hildene, Manchester, 362-1788

Orvis, Manchester, 362-3700

American Museum of Fly Fishing, Manchester, 362-3300

Norman Rockwell Exhibition and Gift Shop, Arlington, 375-6423

Bennington Museum, Bennington, 447-1571

2 ~

Woodstock

From Burlington take I-89 sixty-seven miles to exit 4 in Randolph. The trip starts and ends at the exit in Randolph.

Highlights: *White River Valley with lovely views, Morgan horse country, farmlands, country stores, many covered bridges; Tunbridge World's Fair, Joseph Smith Memorial, Killington and Pico ski areas, edge of the Green Mountain National Forest, birthplace of Calvin Coolidge, Plymouth Notch Historic District.*

The Route

From the interstate, head east on State 66 to Randolph Center and East Randolph, then south on State 14 for a short distance, looking for an unmarked town road from East Randolph to Tunbridge. In Tunbridge take State 110 south to South Royalton and State 14 to State 107 in Bethel. Continue through Stockbridge, then pick up State 100 south through Pittsfield and Sherburne. Pass through the junction of US 4 and State 100, then head south on State 100 to the Coolidge birthplace. From there, go north on State 100A to US 4, then east to Woodstock. Return to Randolph on State 12 through

Barnard and Bethel. The trip is 105 miles long and will take at least three hours without stops.

This drive through south central Vermont and the White River Valley runs through trim towns and sleepy valleys, up mountains and over rivers. It offers a fine view of small-town New England life, replete with no-nonsense general stores, verdant town greens, columned town halls, and simple white church spires.

Economic contrast is pronounced in this region. In tiny, manicured Woodstock, you might spot part-time resident Michael J. Fox eating one table over from the town's best-known benefactors, the Rockefellers. In the country just a few miles away, wealth is defined by the width of your trailer, the number of channels your satellite dish can pull, and the top speed of your snowmobile, or sled, as they are called hereabouts.

Begin in Randolph Center, turning east off the interstate. At one time, this pretty village was a contender for state capital. Although it lost out to Montpelier, the wide streets and fine Federal-style mansions give Randolph Center a refined feel.

Justin Morgan, who developed the strong, sturdy Morgan horse, lived here, and the village remains a horsey place with several stables nearby. Randolph Center is also home to Vermont Technical College, one of five Vermont state colleges. If refreshments are needed, Floyd's General Store is welcoming and conveniently located. From the village, go east on State 66 to East Randolph.

A pleasant view of old hill farms stretches out before the road, with snowmobile trails running through the fields in winter, and cows out ambling through the pastures in summer. As the road climbs the trees grow in close and the area begins to feel quite remote. Weathered buildings and collapsed barns are reminders of the harsh New England weather, as are the rutted roads.

After some plunging views watch for State 14 south, turning right into East Randolph, a humble village. At the East Randolph Country Store, notices boasting the weights of deer killed by local hunters stay up long after hunting season is over.

Longtime Vermonters would say that unpretentious towns such as this are real Vermont. Indeed, so real is this terrain that some of the roads aren't marked, specifically the one to Tunbridge, although all the locals know where it is.

From the country store head south for about a quarter mile, watching for a left turn uphill directly before a tractor dealership. This is your turn. (If you go over the bridge and to the old purple schoolhouse you've gone too far.)

The road to Tunbridge is a steep, very bumpy eight miles. In fact, this road will define frost heaves better than any dictionary. For the record, frost heaves are dips and bumps in the asphalt that are caused by freezes, thaws, and moisture. But the bounce factor is quickly outweighed by the beauty of the views, especially at the top of the hill, where the trees open up onto a panorama of mountains and valley farms.

Come down the hill, past a cemetery, and toward a farm. Keep heading right, past a run-down but marvelously detailed Victorian on the left, and take a right turn onto State 110 south in the direction of Tunbridge.

The river that runs along the road is the White River, First Branch. In the vicinity there are also a Second and a Third Branch, as well as "the Stevens Branch." With so many rivers to cross, it's no wonder that this patch of Vermont is a covered bridge gold mine. Between Chelsea and South Royalton alone, there are six. You'll see three of them on your route.

Tunbridge, named for a prominent British viscount in 1761, is a jumble of newer dwellings and handsome old buildings, including the town hall, church, and library. In England during the 1600s and 1700s, a place called Tunbridge Wells was a fashionable resort known for its mineral springs. Strangely, mineral springs were discovered in Vermont's Tunbridge in the early 1800s, attracting many visitors in search of health cures.

Today, however, Tunbridge is a tourist attraction only during four days in September, when 20,000 people flock to the Tunbridge World's Fair. First sponsored by the Union Agricultural Society in 1867, the fair takes place every year in a natural bowl next to the White River. While the location is idyllic, the fair was long known as a rowdy, roughneck event that lived up to its nickname, "Drunkards' Reunion." Today it is more of a family affair, with beer drinking confined to specific tents. Among the many old-fashioned events are horse pulls, fiddlers' contests, buggy racing, and livestock displays.

Leaving Tunbridge, the views are picturesque. The winding road opens up on a new scene around every curve, sometimes of farms, or ridges, or craggy trees growing up close against the river.

As you arrive in South Royalton, cross the old steel bridge for a quick tour of this town developed between 1848 and 1853 as a freight depot for the Vermont Central Railway.

Most of the buildings surrounding the town green are part of an eighty-building historic district that warrants a look-see. Vermont's only law school, established in 1972, has helped to gentrify the place. There are several restaurants and inns, including the student-hangout Hannah's Cafe. After touring South Royalton, go back across the bridge and turn right for a quick trip to the Joseph Smith Memorial in Sharon.

Smith, founder of the Mormon Church, lived the first ten years of his life in Sharon. He was born on December 23, 1805, on his grandfather's farm, and although his family left Vermont before he had his first vision, his birthplace is marked with a 38 1/2-foot shaft of granite, as well as a museum and chapel. Each foot in the monument marks a year in Smith's life, which ended with his murder in Carthage, Illinois, in 1844. The site is open year-round. Admission is free.

From Sharon, go back toward South Royalton, this time heading north on State 14 through Royalton. Two miles north of Royalton, go west on State 107, passing under the interstate on the way to Bethel. At the junction of State 14 and State 107 you'll see the Vermont Sugar House Restaurant. It provides both the souvenir fix and sugar fix, with its highly commercial façade, accessorized by chain-saw carvings, and its many maple products, including incredibly sweet maple candy.

Continue on State 107 through Bethel and toward Gaysville. In the winter, you'll start seeing cars with skis on this road as they approach the Killington and Pico ski areas. Chalets, log cabins, and inns start to crop up, including the very quaint Greenhurst Inn, an old Queen Anne Victorian mansion in Bethel.

In the summer, enjoy the fine views and watch on the right-hand side for a popular roadside restaurant, Tozier's. Every year, carloads of kids and tourists head for the white-and-green building tucked into the bend of the road, with tall trees offering shade on hot days. Tozier's serves standard fare at affordable prices all summer: hamburgers, hot dogs, malts, fries, and the usual variations.

From Tozier's the road is braced in by trees and mountain on one side and a band of water on the other. In Stockbridge, watch for the River Echo Morgan Horse Farm on the left. Winter and summer, you'll see the sturdy, strong horses in their paddock. Visitors are welcome to look or buy.

Stockbridge, tiny though it may be, is home to one of Vermont's most high-tech companies: Advanced Animations, Inc. From the road, you can see the flag and the red barnlike building that houses a Disneyesque crowd of automated, often life-size characters created for movies, mall displays, and fairs.

After Advanced Animations watch for the turnoff to State 100 south, heading for Pittsfield. Several gift shops line the approach to Pittsfield, a very well-maintained, ski-friendly town with several inns. Suggestions: Swiss Farm Lodge and Pittsfield Inn, located in the center of the village on the green. On the way out of Pittsfield, eager skiers will get their first glimpse of nirvana: the white ribbons of trails cutting swaths on the mountains at Killington.

From Pittsfield south, the road follows the western edge of the Green Mountain National Forest. At the "Welcome to Sherburne" sign the narrow road starts going up. Chalets and inns interrupt the birch and evergreen forest; out-of-state license plates are the rule. Cross-country skiers glide along trails across from Gifford Woods State Park. In summer the park offers camping and hiking on the Appalachian Trail. As State 100 nears the intersection with US 4, development thickens and you are in real ski country.

Killington is the largest ski area in the East, spreading over six mountains. Killington itself is the second highest peak in Vermont, at 4,241 feet. The ski area also likes to boast that it offers skiing until May and even June, thanks to its unequalled snowmaking operation. But beware—this spring fling often consists of one trail.

Pico, just down the road, is smaller and sometimes less crowded during peak season, when thousands of skiers practice their turns on the slopes. Inns are sprinkled all along State 100 and US 4, as well as the six-mile access road to Killington. Skiers also take lodging in Woodstock, twenty miles away, and Rutland, eleven miles away.

While this area is most visited in the winter, it's also popular in the summer, when sporting events and concerts are scheduled. The Killington Golf Course offers one of the most challenging and picturesque courses in the state.

The Killington Gondola runs to the summit on weekends in August and then during mid-September, when the foliage starts to change. For another summer excursion, Pico offers an alpine slide from late June to Labor Day.

Any time of year, it's a pleasant drive straight down State 100 along the Black River to Plymouth Union. Turn left on State 100A, and drive a mile to the Plymouth Notch Historic District.

America's thirtieth president, Calvin Coolidge, was born in the tiny mountain hamlet that today seems to exist in the early 1920s or so. The austere natural beauty and simple white clapboard village echo the frugal, no-nonsense ethic that Coolidge epitomized. He was born on his father's farm in 1872, and even after he embarked on his illustrious political career, he always found time to return there.

It was at the homestead that the visiting vice-president was awakened from a sound sleep in August of 1923 and told that President Warren G. Harding had died of an embolism in San Francisco. The senior Coolidge swore in his son.

During his presidency Coolidge cultivated the image of a laconic Yankee farmer. But he was not merely a simple farmer; when photographed "doing chores" in Plymouth, his fine linen shirts were often visible beneath a borrowed farmer's smock.

The Plymouth Notch Historic District encompasses several buildings, including the general store, which was operated by the father of the president. The site is open from spring through foliage season (mid-May to mid-October) and closed for the winter.

When you're ready to leave Plymouth, head north on State 100A to the junction of US 4 and turn east. It's eight miles to Woodstock, past inns, antique shops, and the occasional factory outlet store. Near Woodstock, watch for the farmers' market next to the office of the local newspaper, the *Vermont Standard*.

Woodstock has been a playground for the wealthy since the late nineteenth century. It continues to attract hordes of tourists, who ogle the well-preserved eighteenth- and nineteenth-century architecture surrounding the elliptical green at the heart of the village. To this day, some tourists confuse Vermont's Woodstock with the New York state version, where the infamous three-day rock music festival took place in 1969. You won't hear many electric guitars in this town; the cautious local selectmen are quite particular about what will and will not be allowed here.

In fact, the conservative townsfolk rebuffed Hollywood producers when they wanted to film the movie *Peyton Place* here many years ago. Zoning laws are still strict—every dot and tittle must be approved.

To that end millionaire Laurance Rockefeller himself picked up the tab for burying the power lines at a cost of more than $100,000. He and his wife, Mary French Rockefeller, own the posh Woodstock Inn and a secluded mansion on Elm Street. Good luck asking for directions to the Rockefeller estate: Loyal locals know just where it is but generally guard their patrons' privacy.

Take a walking tour—you can sign up at the information booth on the town green—or browse through the shops and galleries and have a bite at Bentley's, a popular watering hole. If you have time for a short detour, drive the six miles east on US 4 to Quechee Gorge, a spectacular 165-foot chasm known as Vermont's Grand Canyon. There are picnic grounds, tent sites, and trails leading to the floor of the gorge, where you can even take a dip in the chilly river. Rock climbers beware: You'll pay a $500 fee if rescuers are required to bail you out.

Return to Woodstock and head out of town on Elm Street past the Woodstock Historical Society. You'll pass the First

Congregational Church, where the Rockefellers were married. The church bell was cast by the Paul Revere foundry. After you cross the Ottaquechee River, watch for glimpses of the Rockefeller mansion on the left, although it's well protected from prying eyes by a tall hedge and trees.

Leaving town, you'll see signs for the Billings Farm & Museum. The museum, open daily from May through September, offers a thorough look at nineteenth-century farm life, with animals, exhibits, tools, and farm products.

A bit farther on, you can take a short side trip to Suicide Six ski area, where the first ski tow in the United States went into operation in 1934.

Leaving Woodstock behind, State 12 takes you north ten miles to Barnard. Development gives way to farmland and forest, and the tourist population thins drastically. The small hamlet of Barnard was the home of newspaper columnist Dorothy Thompson. As such, it became a country getaway for many famous politicians and writers in the 1940s. Thompson and her last husband—the one after Sinclair Lewis—are both buried in Barnard.

Just north of Barnard look to the west for Mount Hunger, elevation 2,360 feet. The mountain got its name, it is said, after two men got lost and starved to death there.

Continuing north, it's eight miles to Bethel, a pleasant riverside village and the first town created by the independent Republic of Vermont. Then it's eight miles of charming countryside along the banks of the Third Branch of the White River to Randolph. If you're passing through on a summer evening, you're in for a treat about midway between Bethel and Randolph. Pull into the Randall Drive-in—a classic, and one of the few left in Vermont—and enjoy the show.

Randolph is a friendly, unpretentious town with shops, a few inns and restaurants, including Lupine's, a tidy place

Christmas at the Billings Farm & Museum

with a green-striped awning and lace curtains. The Chandler
Music Hall and Gallery stages concerts and theater.

For lodging, consider the lovely Three Stallion Inn on a
scenic overlook at the edge of town. It adjoins the Green
Mountain Stock Farm, once the principal breeding ground of

the Morgan horse. The views are stunning, and the inn offers riding, tennis, hiking, swimming, mountain biking, and cross-country skiing.

I-89 is just a few miles from the inn. You'll know you're leaving Randolph when you see two oversized whale tails rising up from the ground in what must be one of Vermont's more bizarre sculptures.

In the Area

All phone numbers are in area code 802.

Hannah's Cafe, South Royalton, 763-2626

Vermont Sugar House Restaurant, Royalton, 763-8809

Greenhurst Inn, Bethel, 234-9497

Tozier's, Bethel, 234-9400

Swiss Farm Lodge, Pittsfield, 746-8341

Pittsfield Inn, Pittsfield, 746-8943

Killington Golf Course, Killington, 422-4100

Plymouth Notch Historic District, Plymouth Notch, 672-3650

Billings Farm & Museum, Woodstock, 457-2355

Randolph Chamber of Commerce, Randolph, 728-9027

Three Stallion Inn, Randolph, 800-424-5575

For information about Killington Gondola, Pico Alpine Slide, and more lodging and restaurants, call the Killington and Pico Areas Association, Killington, 775-7070.

3 ~

Gap Country

From Burlington take US 7 thirty-two miles south to Middlebury. The trip begins in Middlebury and ends on the east side of the Green Mountain range in Waitsfield.

Highlights: *Green Mountains and some of the highest elevations in the state, classic New England towns, spectacular views; hiking, picnicking, fishing, skiing; Robert Frost Interpretive Trail, Middlebury College and Bread Loaf campus.*

The Route

The seventy-five-mile trip is slow going and will take at least three hours without stops. From Middlebury head south on US 7 to East Middlebury, pick up State 125 and head east up the mountains to Ripton. On the other side pick up State 100 north and continue toward Warren. Shortly before Warren village, turn left at the sign for Lincoln Gap and cross the mountains again, descending into Lincoln. From there head toward Bristol, and then north on State 17, bound for Appalachian Gap. Conclude your trip in Waitsfield, the heart of Mad River ski country, just a few minutes from I-89.

It is no accident that going to the mountain has in so many cultures been an occasion for contemplation and revelation. Whether you're in a contemplative mood or just looking for panoramic views, this serpentine route through the Green Mountain National Forest will satisfy.

It leads through some of the highest elevations in Vermont, and certainly through the densest concentration of consistently high peaks, combining striking lookouts, rich forests, valley-bottom farms, tumbling waterfalls, and secluded villages.

Check the brakes and be prepared to drive over the Green Mountains three times: through Middlebury Gap, Lincoln Gap, and Appalachian Gap. In winter, check the weather before setting out, and you'll have to forgo Lincoln Gap, which closes when the snow flies. In summer, it's not to be missed.

Middlebury has all the features of a classic New England town: trim white clapboard homes, a lush village green with gazebo, and an old-fashioned soda fountain right across the street. Middlebury College, founded in 1800, enriches the community culturally and aesthetically.

Middlebury College's intellectual sobriety resonates in the many impressive stone buildings that dot the campus. Check out the new arts center, or take a stroll through the Johnson Gallery, where Vermont artists are likely to be exhibited alongside works by Auguste Rodin and Medardo Rosso in the permanent collection.

If you need sustenance before going into the mountains, stop in at Woody's, a funky restaurant overlooking Otter Creek, or pick up fresh bread and gourmet picnic supplies at the Otter Creek Bakery, located on College Street. Then it's off to East Middlebury on US 7, watching for the left turn on State 125 about four miles out of town.

State 125, an eastbound, one-lane mountain road, leads up to Middlebury Gap and straight into the heart of Robert Frost country, taking motorists directly past the unassuming cabin he called home for twenty-three summers.

First, admire the quaint bed and breakfasts in East Middlebury, including the now famous Waybury Inn, with its cozy front porch and homey rockers. Fans of the television show "Newhart" will recognize the exterior from the show's opening credits. Although the sitcom was filmed elsewhere, many "Newhart" fans have made the pilgrimage to the fifteen-room inn, perhaps half-expecting to cross paths with Daryl and Daryl, the plaid-shirted woodchucks of "yup" and "nope" fame.

"Woodchuck," of course, is the Vermont expression for rural dweller, as opposed to "flatlander," which refers to anyone born—or ever having lived—anywhere else in the world, flat or not.

As State 125 ascends into the foothills, the sun filters through the trees and sparkles on the surface of the Middlebury River. Try the fishing, wading, or picnicking, but don't let the driver get too distracted: The sharp corners and narrow lanes require undivided attention.

In tiny Ripton, about four miles up the hill, buy some penny candy at the old Ripton Country Store and admire the handsome white churches. Farther up, watch for the Robert Frost Interpretive Trail on the right. Located just a mile from the cabin where Frost summered, the mile-long trail is a pleasant excursion into nature and poetry over landscape that Frost once trod himself. The trail meanders through meadow, swamp, and forest, with placards bearing Frost's verse at intervals along the way. The experience offers Frost at his best: on nature, in nature.

Back on State 125, you'll see the Robert Frost Wayside Rest Area with its picnic tables, barbecue grills, and water

Stop in at a country store

pump. The pine-needle carpet smells wonderful and the trees provide deep, cool shade.

The many references to Frost on this route make it seem like one long historic district for the United States and Vermont poet laureate, who died in 1963. Frost is a hero to many Vermonters for his ability to versify New England life. Not surprisingly, the old-timers who live in this area have many anecdotes about the wise, white-haired bard, who, they say, was alternately kind and cantankerous. Many people made the trek here during Frost's lifetime to talk with him or interview him. Occasionally he consented, though by the end of his life he was plain tired of talking about himself. "I don't get seasick," he told one journalist. "I get me sick."

Frost and many other famous writers have taught their craft at the Bread Loaf Writers' Conference, the campus of which is intersected by State 125, just a few miles from the Robert Frost Wayside Rest Area. Owned by Middlebury College, Bread Loaf's lush mountaintop campus is lined with neat yellow and white clapboard buildings. In summer, the endless green lawns are dotted with white Adirondack chairs.

The campus is used for summer school and conferences, the aforementioned writers' conference being the most famous, both for the teaching and the lively cocktail parties. William Styron, John Irving, and Eudora Welty are among the many notable writers who have made the trek to Bread Loaf. While new writers are occasionally "discovered" at the ten-day conference, no doubt their writing would pale against a factual account of the legendary drinking and fraternizing that the literary set is said to engage in each summer.

Continue on State 125, watching for the Middlebury Snow Bowl on the right. The small ski area, also owned by the college, has three Poma lifts and a chairlift and is a friendly, out-of-the-way place to ski in winter.

Above the Snow Bowl, you'll climb into Middlebury Gap, elevation 2,149 feet. The views from the top are stunning, and even prettier on the way down the other side. Deep forest crowds the road on both sides, parting periodically for stunning views of the next range to the east.

A couple miles down from the summit, you'll see signs on the left for Texas Falls. Follow the access road upstream and listen for the low roar of the falls slicing through the gloom of the forest, about a mile from State 125. Footbridges arch over violent torrents of water, and huge faces of wet rock glisten with green moss. Swimming is not allowed, but the picnicking is fine.

Ski chalets begin appearing in clumps on the last three miles of State 125. Many are owned by out-of-staters, who form ski clubs and take to the slopes on winter weekends at nearby Sugarbush or Mad River Glen.

At the junction with State 100, you have arrived in Hancock, little more than a cluster of old buildings and an intersection. Consider a stop at the Vermont Home Bakery, located in the old Hancock Hotel building. Renovation has erased any signs of this building's former life as a hotel, and lodging is no longer available, but the inexpensive down-home fare—running to meatloaf, lasagne, pie, and milkshakes—makes it popular with the locals, and you can browse the gift shop for Vermont wines, hams, and chocolates.

From Hancock, turn north on State 100. For the next twenty miles or so, the road slices through narrow swaths of cornfield and swamp, or past walls of forested mountain and rock.

Heading north toward Granville, the White River proper keeps you company. There's not much to it up here near its source on the western fringes of the Connecticut River watershed. In places the countryside is desolate, with derelict houses long abandoned on the edge of the forest, roofs sunken and slumped, porches rotted.

The little town of Granville sprawls about a woodworking factory at its hub. Stop and shop for the local product at the Vermont Wood Specialties shop or Vermont Only Village Store. Both offer a range of wood products, from bowls and spoons to chairs. Watch for inexpensive factory seconds, and check out the weekend tours of the Vermont Wood Specialties factory.

Continuing north, say good-bye to the White River, which doglegs west into the mountains toward its fountainhead somewhere near the summit of 3,823-foot Bread Loaf Mountain. Closer to Warren, former farmhouses that now serve as ski clubs stand abandoned during summer months, waiting for winter weekends when they'll be packed to the rafters with enthusiastic skiers from Connecticut, New York, New Jersey, Quebec, and beyond.

Houses are generally few and far between. Farmland surrenders to deep forest at Granville Gulch, where the road pries its way between the mountain ranges, crowded on either side by dense stands of hardwood and fir.

You can pull over near Moss Glen Falls, where a quick mountain stream tumbles out of the forest on the side of 3,580-foot Mount Roosevelt. Near the falls, State 100 begins a gentle descent toward Warren, picking up the humble beginnings of the Mad River.

In Warren, about fourteen miles from Granville, you'll see signs for a sharp left up into the mountains toward Lincoln Gap, but you might first choose to quickly explore Warren village, with its requisite millpond and covered bridge and a cluster of houses, most of them the upscale properties of ski community members. A small general store marks the center of town, serving up fine sandwiches and picnic fare and a decent selection of wine. You might want to grab something here for picnicking at the top of Lincoln Gap.

Covered bridge and millpond on the Mad River

Climbing west out of the Mad River Valley, the road turns to dirt, winding upward past handsome houses and pleasant countryside. Massive maples line the road, spreading their branches high above tumbledown stone walls on either side. Higher up, the road turns back to pavement to begin the ascent in earnest.

As you near the top, the Lincoln Gap road takes on a mystical quality. Switchbacks ease you up the impossible grade through damp, mossy forests. Beneath an unbroken canopy of trees—mostly beech up here—ferns and mushrooms grow in the soft, soggy leafmold of the forest floor. Periodically, the trees on the right side of the road part momentarily to reveal tantalizing glimpses of the valley floor, far below, then close in again as you continue upward.

The grade gets steeper still near the top—stay in first gear and slow to a creep—and there's no mistaking the summit, elevation 2,424 (the highest gap in Vermont), where the road takes a sudden and dramatic nosedive down the west side of the divide. You will find places to pull over and enjoy the spectacular views and watch hikers cross the road on the ubiquitous Long Trail. You'll find a particularly good, though small, pull-off just a quarter mile down the west side, providing especially nice views of the town of Lincoln and the Champlain Valley far below. On the way down, the road returns to dirt as the grade evens out a bit.

You'll descend past farms and fields to an intersection at the New Haven River, about four miles from the summit. Turn north toward Lincoln, an out-of-the-way foothills village where New York City gossip columnist Liz Smith goes to escape the Manhattan rat race.

Pressing west from Lincoln, it's four miles to the junction with State 116 and the hamlet of Rocky Dale, and gardeners are in for a treat. The Rockydale Gardens and Nursery may be like none you've ever seen. Its immaculately landscaped grounds go on and on, bordered on the back of the lot by the sudden rise of South Mountain (elevation 2,307), where exposed ledges tumble off the side of the mountain, lyrically planted with an array of groundcovers. There's an exhaustive array of shrubs, trees, and perennials to browse among and a shop where you can ask for advice or look over the charming lawn ornaments.

When you've covered the grounds—it could easily take an hour—you might be ready for a bite to eat. Barely a half mile south of the nursery, you'll see the Squirrel's Nest Restaurant on the right—a casual summery place that looks like a good bet for cheeseburgers and milkshakes—or you can press on toward downtown Bristol. On the way, a curious Bristol landmark guards the roadside. It's a massive boulder on the right side of the road—apparently a monument of the Ice Age—and it has been engraved with the Lord's Prayer and the date, 1891.

Downtown Bristol is charming. Brick and clapboard businesses line a busy little main street—the effect is Small-town New England, USA. Pickup trucks wait outside Mary's Restaurant, a good bet for lunch, judging by its apparent popularity among the locals. Deerleap Books has a fine selection, and the town green, with its gazebo, is a nice place to picnic. Bristol's claim to fame—besides once being "the Coffin-Manufacturing Capital of the United States"—is its annual outhouse race, a Fourth of July spectacle of now legendary stature, owing to its television appearance on the "Today" show.

When it's time to escape the hustle of downtown Bristol, turn back north on State 17 and begin the day's final assault on the mountains.

State 17 follows Baldwin Creek back out into farmland and then up into Appalachian Gap. This mountain pass is used heavily in the winter by skiers from the west side of the range heading over for skiing at the three ski areas on the east side. The state has obliged by carving out a wide road and keeping it clear in the winter. Still, as you can imagine, it takes a hardy vehicle to make it over on a snowy day, even with the state plows hard at work.

The road winds upward on generous switchbacks through dense forest. The mountains on either side are named for Battle of Bennington hero General John Stark (to the south, elevation 3,662) and his wife, Molly Stark (to the north, elevation 2,967).

There are few houses up here. Near the top, the road makes one last upward sweep toward the summit, a pitch that leaves many cars spinning their wheels helplessly in the snow but affords splendid views up the range to the north. A high mountain pond sparkles in its cradle just below the notch, and then you're at the summit, elevation 2,356, looking out over the Mad River Valley to the east and back over the Champlain Valley to the west. You'll find places to pull over and take in the scenery, and the Long Trail, your old friend by now, is close at hand.

When you're ready to take the plunge down the east side of the ridge, quirky Mad River Glen welcomes you back to ski country. Mad River, owned and operated by the charismatic Betsy Pratt, is a ski area frozen in time. While Vermont's other resorts race to see who can build the fastest lifts and make the most snow and attract the most tourists, Pratt's Mad River contents itself with natural beauty and a laid-back atmosphere. Its motto, "Ski it if you can," is appropriate. Little has been done to impress the will of man upon the rugged terrain, and the absence of any significant amount of snowmaking can create challenging conditions. But when the snow falls in abundance, serious skiers make the pilgrimage, and Mad River's near-antique single chair groans under the weight of delighted skiers. It's a cozy throwback to the days before out-of-state investors and huge corporations turned skiing in Vermont into a matter of profits and losses.

A few miles farther, take a right on German Flats Road and explore the valley's other conventional ski areas, Sugarbush North and Sugarbush Valley. The two have been operated by the same company since Sugarbush purchased the defunct Glenn Ellen ski area in the seventies and renamed it. The summit lift at Sugarbush North whisks skiers to the frozen summit of Mount Ellen, elevation 4,135, where the views are spectacular: north to Burlington, west to Lake Champlain and the Adirondacks, east on a clear day to the White Mountains a hundred miles distant. Sugarbush North, like Killington, takes advantage of its northern exposure to prolong the ski season well into spring. Even as the trees are beginning to leaf out on the valley floor, hard-core skiers are still enjoying the last vestiges of the season, dodging bare patches and soaking up the sun as it turns a season's worth of snow to mud and water.

A few miles beyond Sugarbush North you'll hit the Sugarbush access road. Turn right for a half-mile cruise up to Sugarbush Valley Ski Resort, now known more commonly as Sugarbush South. At the base of the parking lot, turn left up an unmarked road that turns to dirt. It's a pleasant back road through the forest and back down the hill to State 100. You'll pass the eleventh, twelfth, and thirteenth fairways of the Sugarbush Golf Club. Stop in if you're ready for a go at one of Vermont's toughest courses, but bring plenty of balls, because the fairways are notoriously tight and the woods are deep.

A few miles farther down the road you'll come out on State 100 near Warren village. You're just a few hundred yards north of the Lincoln Gap road you took earlier. But before you call it a day, cruise north along the Mad River and check out Irasville and Waitsfield. You'll find boutiques and art galleries to explore and plenty of restaurants for weary travelers.

In the Area

All phone numbers are in area code 802.

Calvy's, Middlebury, (no phone)

Otter Creek Bakery, Middlebury, 388-3371

Woody's Restaurant, Middlebury, 388-4182

Middlebury Inn, Middlebury, 388-4961

Waybury Inn, East Middlebury, 388-4015

Ripton Country Store, Ripton, 388-7328

Middlebury College Snow Bowl, Hancock, 388-4356

Vermont Home Bakery, Hancock, 767-4976

Vermont Wood Specialties, Granville, 767-4711

Vermont Only Village Store, Granville, 767-4711

Rockydale Gardens and Nursery, Bristol, 453-2782

Squirrel's Nest Restaurant, Bristol, 453-6042

Mary's Restaurant, Bristol, 453-2432

Deerleap Books, Bristol, 453-5684

Mad River Glen Ski Area, Fayston, 496-3553

Sugarbush Resort, Warren, 583-2381

Sugarbush Golf Club, Warren, 583-2722

The Warren Store, Warren 496-3864

4 ~

Barre-
Montpelier

From **Burlington** take I-89 south thirty-five miles to exit 8 in Montpelier. From Boston take I-93 north to Concord, New Hampshire; I-89 north to Vermont exit 8, Montpelier. This trip begins and ends in Montpelier.

Highlights: *State capital with tours and interesting architecture; panoramic views, farms and farm stands, granite quarries; picnicking, swimming; New England Culinary Institute, Vermont College, Hope Cemetery.*

The Route

From Montpelier, take State 12 to north Worcester, then town roads east through Maple Corner, Kent's Corner, and Calais to State 14. Take State 14 south to Barre, detour to the Barre granite quarries, then continue south on State 14 to East Brookfield. Take State 65 west to Brookfield proper, then back to East Brookfield, then south on State 14 to East Randolph. From East Randolph, take town roads east to an intersection with State 110, just south of Chelsea. Take State 110 north through Chelsea village and Washington to US 302 in East

Barre, then US 302 west to Barre. This trip is eighty-five miles long and takes at least 2 1/2 hours without stops.

Montpelier, with its government buildings, museum, and thriving Main Street, is as good a place as any to get a feel for the character of the state. Then you're off to explore the dirt roads and country lanes that wind through the hills and farms just north of town. From there, the back door into Barre opens upon the truly wonderful Hope Cemetery, a sprawling hillside graveyard scattered with one-of-a-kind tombstones and crypts that serve as fitting monuments to Barre's stone-cutting heritage.

Main Street in Barre takes you up to the mountain-top quarries, where abandoned quarries and mountains of rubble have transformed the landscape. Then you'll go into the countryside—and what countryside. The west side of Orange County is a rural fairy kingdom, frozen in a time when hillside and valley-bottom farms were the rule and paved roads the exception. On the shore of Sunset Lake, tiny Brookfield hides among the maple trees at the east end of its curious Floating Bridge—the longest pontoon span in the country. Then the Second Branch of the White River leads the way south through the countryside to North Randolph and East Randolph, where dirt lanes cross the ridge to the charming hamlet of Chelsea, Orange County seat, and the enchanting Washington Gulf marks the way back to Barre.

In a state where small is beautiful, Vermont's capital is no exception. Montpelier, the heart of this central Vermont loop, is the nation's smallest capital. It clings to the banks of the Winooski River, side by side with its bigger, grittier cousin, Barre (pronounced "barry"), linked by a five-mile stretch of strip development but otherwise surrounded by unsullied countryside.

The two make a charismatic couple: Montpelier the dignified, white-collar college town, a small, quiet community where residents go about the business of governing the state; Barre the muscular younger brother, a rough-and-tumble quarry town with a solid work ethic and a few rough edges.

Perhaps fittingly for the Green Mountain State, her statehouse is perched hard against the base of a small, rugged mountain. Against this striking backdrop, Ceres, Greek goddess of agriculture, rules from atop her gold-domed temple. Naturally, the statehouse is made of granite, hauled by oxen teams from Barre quarries ten miles away. The building itself is the third to stand on that spot. The original was built in 1808 on land granted by the citizens of Montpelier, but the legislators, who are said to have made a hobby out of carving up their wooden desks with penknives during particularly monotonous legislative sessions, soon outgrew these cramped quarters. In 1836, the building was demolished to make way for a far grander affair of granite hewn from the mountainsides of nearby Graniteville. The new building, its architecture inspired by the temples of ancient Greece, was lost to a horrible fire on a bitterly cold, windy night in 1857, and the present-day structure was rebuilt on what was left when the ashes cooled.

Today, twenty-minute tours of the handsome old building are available from July through October, free of charge. Tours are not given during the legislative session, which runs from January until about May.

On the tour, take note of the fine antique furniture and of the prehistoric sea fossils embedded in the parquet marble floor of the atrium. You'll see a fine marble statue of Ethan Allen, Vermont's Revolutionary War hero, by nineteenth-century sculptor Larkin Mead, but take this likeness with a grain of historical salt: No portraits of Allen existed, and Mead had only his imagination to guide him as he fashioned his version of the original Green Mountain Boy.

In the nearby Pavilion building, a replica of the original Victorian Hotel built to accommodate legislators, visit the

Vermont Museum for a fascinating overview of Vermont's history and its fiercely independent heritage. Keep your eye peeled for the governor, who is likely to be at work upstairs in the governor's working office. A ceremonial office is still located in the statehouse.

Allow time to explore the downtown area. The southern end of Main Street is dominated by the handsome City Hall, a Renaissance Revival affair reminiscent of the municipal palazzos of Tuscany with its square clock tower soaring skyward from three granite arches.

Take a drive up East State Street to the hilltop campus of Vermont College. It's a fine collection of handsome brick buildings around a tidy campus green, anchored by another architectural treasure, the stately College Hall, a French Second Empire structure dating to 1868. The school was originally home to the Vermont Methodist Seminary, which closed its doors in 1947. Vermont College is now part of Norwich University, the nation's oldest private military academy, based in the nearby textile town of Northfield.

Despite its diminutive size, you can eat well in Montpelier, thanks to the presence of the highly regarded New England Culinary Institute. Students cut their teeth in a pair of local establishments: the refined Tubbs Restaurant on Elm Street, and its more casual partner a few doors down, the Elm Street Cafe. If you're more in the mood for a slice of Montpelier life, consider the Horn of the Moon Cafe around the corner on Langdon Street. The cafe serves as a meeting place for central Vermont's well-entrenched back-to-the-landers, who sip herbal tea over whole grains and tofu.

From Montpelier, slip north out of town on either Elm Street or Main Street and take State 12 north toward Worcester. Stately city homes fade to farms and countryside a few miles out of town. Resist the urge to stop for a break beside the Wrightsville Dam Reservoir—there's a better opportunity ahead.

In Worcester, seven miles north of downtown Montpelier, turn right onto Worcester Road and head east toward Calais. It's a short and pleasant drive over a forested ridge on a dirt road to a magical country crossroads called Maple Corners, on the shores of Curtis Pond. Two immaculately maintained farms, neither apparently working, flank the south end of Curtis Pond, where the road passes a few yards from the water's edge. Here is your chance to get out and picnic by the water. Just beyond the boat launch you'll find a recreation area located on a tree-lined peninsula that juts out into the pond.

The spot is a favorite with overheated locals in July and August; tourists are fairly rare. By winter, the pond is dotted with ice-fishing shanties. Inside, folks brave the elements to put a few fresh perch on the table.

Maple Corners proper is just a few hundred yards down the road, at a three-way intersection surrounded by trim farm buildings. Take a right, then an immediate left by the general store and post office. Yes, this speck-on-the-map hamlet somehow manages to have its own post office. It's a short drive on more dirt road to Kent's Corner, an equally enchanting and even smaller community than Maple Corners, anchored by a country crossroads and a pair of large, handsome homes, including the 1810 Ira Kent House.

From Kent's Corner it's a couple of miles downhill into the lost valley of Calais, site of the Calais Town Hall ("Official Polling Place") and little else. At the three-way intersection, turn right and follow the stream past a couple of farms and an old schoolhouse in the middle of nowhere, and you'll arrive at State 14.

A church at the crossroads

Back on pavement, consider a stop at the Legare Farm, especially if it's harvest season. The family-owned vegetable farm/nursery has wonderful produce and a solid selection of annuals and perennials. From the trim brick and clapboard Federal farmhouse and barns, carefully tended fields spread out along the Kingsbury Branch river valley. It's a pleasure to see a vital working farm in the days of corporate farming and California produce.

Farther south, you'll roll into North Montpelier with its millpond and dilapidated Victorian mansion. On winter weekends the locals take to the ice on snowmobiles to see who has the fastest "sled." The scream of two-cylinder engines can be deafening, but the snowsuited contestants plainly enjoy themselves.

From North Montpelier it's a two-mile climb to the top of a ridge that affords panoramic views in all directions. Then you'll descend into East Montpelier. Pass through the blinking yellow light, then look for a left turn across the river, staying on State 14, which goes into Barre the back way.

There's nothing remarkable about the ensuing six-mile stretch of State 14, except that it leads to the entrance of the amazing Hope Cemetery, and there could be no more poetically appropriate gateway to the gritty quarry town of Barre.

The dust-choked stone sheds of Barre killed immigrant stonecutters by the thousands, and here they lie, their graves marked, appropriately, by beautiful monuments. In some cases, stonecutters suffering from silicosis made their own monuments before they died, leaving eerie testament to their life's work. More often, the monuments are the creations of fellow workers.

When the railroads came to Barre late in the nineteenth century, the granite industry boomed, making Barre the granite capital of the world for a time. Immigrants seeking better lives flocked to central Vermont from quarries in Italy, Spain, Scotland, and Scandinavia. In the stone sheds of Websterville and Graniteville, which, unlike those of the Old World, were enclosed against the elements of winter, these skilled blue-collar artists chiseled works of undying beauty from the cold, gray Barre granite, unaware that the thick dust hanging in the air of the unventilated sheds was killing them. Entire families were wiped out by silicosis, and high on a hill overlooking Barre, the lavish monuments of an otherwise simple people bear testimony to their skill.

Hope Cemetery goes on and on, crowded with remarkable works of art, sometimes gaudy, sometimes breathtaking. You'll need hours to explore it thoroughly, but be sure at least to find the crown jewel of the cemetery, the Elia Corti monument, which bears a head-to-toe likeness of the deceased, seated in a thoughtful pose, resplendent in his best suit of clothes.

Leaving Hope Cemetery, you'll descend into Barre on Maple Street, which arrives at an intersection with State 14 and US 302. Here at the intersection, amid urban sprawl and strip development, stands a recently erected monument to Barre's stonecutting heritage, a single immigrant artisan captured with hammer and chisel in hand—fitting tribute to the people of this broad-shouldered town.

Take a left onto Main Street and it's a mile or so to the town square, in this case a triangle ringed by a handsome collection of old buildings. You'll see the Barre Opera House and, up on a hill overlooking the park, the proud Spaulding Graded School, a Richardsonian Romanesque affair with a statue of the poet Bobby Burns out front, lovingly erected, one presumes, by members of the city's Scottish population.

Take a turn around the park for a close look at the architecture, and then you're off again, heading south on State 14. After a mile or so, look for a left turn onto Quarry Road. It's a steep climb past stone sheds, toward the heart and soul of Barre, the quarries. You'll pass Thunder Road, an aptly named auto raceway that packs in fans by the thousands on sultry summer nights. A mile or two farther up, go left at a three-way intersection, following signs to the quarries. You'll pass the Rock of Ages stone shed. Rock of Ages is the largest monument maker in the United States, and its visitors center offers a fine history of the industry.

Soon you're in among the quarries, high up on Cobble and Millstone hills. In places the road passes within a few yards of the plunging maws where "quarry rats" armed with sledge hammers and hand chisels dismantled entire hillsides. Overhead, the sky is bisected and dissected by winching cables that spread like tentacles from towering pylons. Mountains of rubble, piled here and there among the houses, churches, and trees, bear testimony to the boom years of the

1890s, when as many as seventy working quarries made Barre the granite supplier to a nation. Some of the heaps are so old that forests have begun to reclaim them. The overall effect is of an industrial wasteland, but a fascinating one.

After you've explored the area, work your way back down the hill to State 14. From the urban milieu and turbulent past of Barre, it's a quick plunge back into the serene countryside that surrounds it. State 14 knifes between a pair of mountain ranges, through Williamstown and into East Brookfield, where the terrain opens up and gives way to valley-bottom farms. The countryside that lies ahead is as beautiful as any in Vermont.

Begin by taking State 65 west out of East Brookfield. It's a two-mile climb up the west side of the valley into Brookfield proper, an idyllic and seemingly forgotten hillside farming community. Brookfield's claim to fame is Floating Bridge, a curious feat of engineering that spans what is officially known as Sunset Lake, but is known locally by a variety of other names. Floating Bridge was originally built in 1820, but the existing version is the seventh. It is said to be buoyed by 380 barrels—the lake is too deep to permit a conventional bridge—and is open to both car and foot travel, except in winter, when motorists must find an alternate route if they hope to get to Randolph.

Floating Bridge is popular with anglers and swimmers by summer, and makes an excellent vantage point in late January for the annual ice harvest festival, when locals try their hands at a skill rendered obsolete by the invention of the refrigerator. In summer you can take your lunch on the deck of the adjacent Fork Shop Restaurant, housed in a former pitchfork factory. A few yards away, the Green Trails Inn offers moderately priced rooms in a sprawling 1790s farmhouse. It's a splendid base for cyclers in the summer and cross-country skiers in the winter.

If you can tear yourself away, leave Brookfield and head back down the hill. In East Brookfield, continue south on State 14 to East Randolph. It's six miles of breathtaking scenery dotted by 200-year-old farms along the Second Branch of the White River. In East Randolph, a tiny four-corners farm community, look for a left turn up the hill toward Chelsea.

As the road winds up the east side of the valley, you'll soon notice a change in the character of the farms, as valley-bottom spreads give way to hardscrabble hill farms. Such operations are obviously less prosperous, but no less charming, even where they have become victims of neglect. Weathered barns stand close beside the road, often directly across from the farmhouse. The effect is to give motorists the uneasy feeling that they are driving through someone's yard.

About six miles from East Randolph, look for a three-way intersection beside a caving-in Victorian house that is still inhabited despite its ruinous appearance. Take a right, and it's a mile to State 110, which follows the First Branch of the White River north toward Chelsea.

Despite its isolation, Chelsea, the shire town of Orange County, is a vital little community with a strong sense of identity. Among former residents, it lays claim to the enterprising Hood brothers, one of whom founded the H. P. Hood dairy corporation. The little village features not one but two tree-lined town greens, which carry the eye up a gentle slope to a trio of venerable buildings: the United Church, the Chelsea Public School, and the Orange County Courthouse. The town's original post office, built in 1806, still stands and operates, as do a pair of nearly identical brick buildings built about 1818, one of which still bears advertising as "The Old Hood Store."

Take a slow spin around the town greens and then continue north. Just outside of town, cows graze on hillsides so steep that it's a marvel anyone ever thought to clear them. The river narrows to a brook and disappears into hills. Then the mountains close in on either side, and the heavily forested road makes its way up through Washington Gulf and into Washington, yet another crossroads hamlet.

Descending back into East Barre, there are panoramic views across a lonely windswept ridge. State 110 takes you back into granite country at the junction of US 302, where you'll turn west and follow Jail Brook into Barre.

Bobby Burns welcomes you back to Barre at the town green. Make the short hop to Montpelier for dinner at Tubbs, and you'll be ready to call it a day.

In the Area

All phone numbers are in area code 802.

Tubbs Restaurant, Montpelier, 229-9202

Elm Street Cafe, Montpelier, 223-3188

Horn of the Moon Cafe, Montpelier, 223-2895

Legare Farm Market, Berlin, 476-5037

Thunder Road International Speedbowl, Barre, 479-2151

Green Trails Inn, Brookfield, 276-3412

Fork Shop Restaurant, Brookfield, no phone

5 ~

The

Vergennes

Route:
Big Sky
Vermont

From Burlington take US 7 south twenty miles to Vergennes. The trip starts and ends in Vergennes.

Highlights: *Apple country, antiques; boating, tennis, swimming, hiking, golf; Lake Champlain, Basin Harbor Maritime Museum, Chimney Point, Museum of Native American and French Heritage, University of Vermont's Morgan Horse Farm, Dead Creek Wildlife Management Area.*

The Route

From Vergennes, follow Otter Creek to Basin Harbor on Lake Champlain, then head south to Panton. Stay hard by the lake on Shore Road, which merges with State 17 near Chimney Point. At Chimney Point, go south on State 125 for three miles, turning right onto an unmarked road that heads back toward the lake and turns to dirt for most of the twelve-mile lakeside drive to Larabees Point. In Larabees Point, turn right on State 74, then immediately left on State 73 to Orwell. At Orwell, take State 22A north to Shoreham. In Shoreham, turn east on State 74 to Cornwall. One mile north of Cornwall, bear left on Cider Hill Road and take back roads north through Weybridge to State 17. Turn west on State 17 back to 22A in Addison, then north to Vergennes. The trip is seventy-four miles, much of it on dirt roads. The total time is at least 2 1/2 hours.

This is apple country, breathtaking in the spring and delicious in the fall. Be sure to stop and munch a few apples while you enjoy the views of the Adirondacks, Lake Champlain shore, and the fertile farm country. Visit the Museum of Native American and French Heritage, add some antiques to your collection, or stroke the velvet nose of a sturdy bay Morgan horse.

The southwestern chunk of Vermont is the resting place for Lake Champlain: The farther south you go, the smaller and thinner the lake gets, until it fades to a trickle. At many points on this route, the lake looks narrow enough to swim, and the Adirondacks loom big and blue, a jagged profile against the sky.

Some of Vermont's most mature and fertile orchards are located in this section of the state, along with processing cooperatives. Every fall, apple pickers from faraway places—many of them Jamaicans—come to harvest the crop, beginning in August and continuing through the first week of November.

In contrast to the rows of neatly planted apple trees, some of the state's largest and flattest farms stretch out here. The expansive, wide open views give southwestern Vermont a distinctively different character from the rest of the state.

Our starting point is Vergennes, which advertises itself as the "smallest city" in America, with roughly 2,300 inhabitants. Vergennes is a charming place with eighty significant buildings that comprise a historic district in the center of the city.

The main street is lined with large, mostly well-maintained Victorian mansions, some of them converted to inns or offices. Buildings of note include the Bixby Memorial Free Library, a pillared, pedimented affair built in the neoclassical style in 1912.

Vergennes was founded in 1764 and named for a French minister of foreign affairs who supported the Revolutionary War cause. The city originally attracted settlers because of the natural power source at Otter Creek falls on the west end of town. Ships and cannonballs hastily made in Vergennes were used to defeat the British during the War of 1812.

In recent years, the city has languished a bit as the nearby defense contractor, Simmonds Precision, has cut back its work force. But the downtown area is still remarkably attractive, with nary a modern structure in sight.

Attractions include the Kennedy Brothers Factory Marketplace on the edge of town, an old brick factory building brimming with antiques on consignment, as well as new wood products, crafts, and edibles.

The Rokeby Museum, three miles north of Vergennes in Ferrisburgh, was the home of nineteenth-century author and illustrator Rowland E. Robinson. The house was also an important stop in the underground railway for fugitive slaves.

Restaurants include the Vermont Pasta Restaurant and Bar, featuring moderately priced homemade pasta on the green in the center of town, or the nearby Main Street Bistro, which offers mostly French bistro fare in an intimate setting.

After exploring Vergennes, head out of town on State 22A. About a half mile from downtown, turn right on an unmarked road. You'll soon pick up Otter Creek and follow it through farm country toward the lake and Basin Harbor Club. The creek is wide and slow, with trees arching over its banks. Sheep and cows graze in nearby pastures and in just a few miles the signs to Basin Harbor appear.

The Inn at Basin Harbor is a popular family resort situated on a beautiful cove. Boating, tennis, swimming, hiking,

A swim is just the ticket on a warm Vermont summer day

and golf keep guests busy. Accommodations include lodges, rooms in the inn, and tiny cottages perched right on the shore. Family activities are plentiful, and private planes arrive and depart from a nearby 3,200-foot airstrip.

At the intersection of the club entrance and Panton Road, you might want to peek into the Lake Champlain Maritime Museum. Housed in a former one-room school, it tells the story of adventure, war, commerce, and formation of the lake.

Turn right onto Panton Road, heading south. Panton, little more than a cluster of stone buildings, appears in five miles. There is a lovely little church on Adams Ferry Road. Leaving Panton village south on Lake Road (unmarked), start keeping an eye out for what the local landscapers and stone-masons refer to as Panton stone, a variety of stone that comes out of the ground in uniformly rectangular chunks.

The locals have put Panton stone to good use—in stone walls, houses, porch steps, and chimneys. It also piles up naturally along the road. The stone houses, especially, are as beautiful as they are sturdy, and you'll see plenty of them as you head south. Near Vergennes, most of them have been gentrified, and are no longer working farms or orchards but homes of Burlington and Middlebury commuters. The road winds up to and away from the lake as it makes its way south. Stately homes command stunning views across the lake to the Adirondacks. Farther south, it's refreshing to see that the land returns to working farmland, with hayfields sloping right down to the shoreline and Holsteins and Jerseys taking lunch in the pastures with no mind for the scenery.

Newcomers to farm country might be surprised to see calves tethered in small, individual huts. Often there is not enough room in the barn for calves, so they are kept safely out of the way in their own small pens.

The farther south you drive, the deeper into apple country you go. On the northern edges of the region, a few of the older orchards appear to be neglected, casualties of rising land prices, or abandoned because their trees bear obsolete varieties of bygone eras. Neglected pastures are divided by tangled remnants of rusted barbed-wire fences, or in some cases, even older and prettier split-rail fences that still look like they could keep the livestock out of the road.

Soon, however, the fields give way to immaculately tended orchards crowded with the very latest in hybridized miniature trees, groaning, in fall, under the weight of their Macs and Cortlands.

Vermont's eighty commercial apple growers produce more than one million bushels a year. Addison County is one of the three major apple regions in the state, due in large part to the warming influence of the lake. To get a closer look at the industry, make time for a rest stop at the enchanting Yankee Kingdom Orchard, where two chubby donkeys, Beau and Flipper, won't be satisfied until you feed them a handful of grain. It's sold for twenty-five cents a handful in gumball-type vending machines right next to their pen.

Beau and Flipper reign benevolently over an enormous working orchard established by a local family in 1911 and now owned by Connecticut transplant Mike Johnston and his wife. You can explore the well-stocked garden nursery and forage in the creaky gift shop for a pleasant lunch of apples, cheese, bread, and cider. Then head across the road to a nearby cluster of picnic tables and enjoy your light repast in the country air.

At Yankee Kingdom, and most Vermont orchards, the tart, crisp McIntosh is the dominant variety. It accounts for almost 70 percent of the state's apple crop, with Cortland, Empire, Paulared, and Delicious rounding out the list.

When you're ready to head out, toss Beau and Flipper a farewell handful and continue south. You'll see a very real slice of Vermont life through here, with working farms, modest homes, and occasional mobile homes, all cast against the fairyland backdrop of lake and mountain.

You'll soon join State 17, nearing the end of its westward journey from the top of the Appalachian Gap forty miles to the east. After a few more miles of farms and fields and stone country homes you'll arrive at the Champlain Bridge, a handsome World War II–era steel span that takes advantage of a narrowing in the lake to link Chimney Point on the Vermont shore with Crown Point in New York.

There's something enchanting about Chimney Point: the monumental bridge, the still lake, the convergence of two states and a couple of handsome houses—one a stately Victorian hard by the water.

You can visit the Museum of Native American and French Heritage, a grand old brick house with sweeping porches that take advantage of the lake views, or stop in for tourist information at the adjoining Addison County Chamber of Commerce. There's a boat launch under the bridge, where you can nose your car right down to the edge of the water and appreciate the seldom-seen underside of the bridge. No trolls here.

Cross the bridge to New York—just to say you did—then come back and continue south on State 125 east. Three miles from the bridge, watch for a right turn that comes shortly after a nice brick farmhouse with pillars at its entrance.

This shore road curves along the lake in places where it's no wider than a quarter mile. New York is within shouting distance to the west. To the east, wide open farmland stretches out under an open sky. Enjoy the vistas and watch for deer, grouse, fox, and birds of prey.

During deer season, usually the second and third week of November, hunters cruise these back roads looking for bucks who feed at the apple orchards. You'll also note with surprise the C-Farr Ranch, a big spread that is home to one of Vermont's few herds of beef cattle. It's as close as Vermont gets to Montana.

So much of Vermont is characterized by smallness—its towns, population, and rocky hill farms. That makes these expansive landscapes all the more striking. The views are marred somewhat by the International Paper Company plant across the lake in Ticonderoga. The plant's smokestacks and sodium lights loom incongruously in an otherwise rural setting. Fortunately, the plant fades from view as the road takes a turn inland and plunges into a mammoth working orchard.

New and old trees are planted in neat rows, descending toward the lake. You'll see a sign for Sentinel Orchards, and the road veers right. Follow it, ignoring a left, and head south

Browse in a country church graveyard

OLN 93 ©

toward Larabees Point. The road runs along a ridge, offering more fine views of Vermont apple country and the shimmering blues of the lake, with mountains hovering over it on the other side.

At the junction of State 74, turn right, then left onto State 73 after about a mile. The lake slips from view and the terrain flattens out again in the five-mile cruise to tiny Orwell.

Orwell sits at the intersection of State 22A and State 73, proud and trim with its big brick Congregational Church, town green, pavilion, stately Victorian homes, and charming bank. The church, brick with enormous white pillars and square clock tower, is one of the oldest in Vermont, and it dominates the village. Take a spin through town, then backtrack to State 22A and go right.

Heading north for Shoreham, wide open fields and big farms spread out over gently rolling terrain that is well suited to dairy farming. That changes abruptly when you leave State 22A in Shoreham and head northeast on State 74. The road climbs up onto a low rocky ridge. Fields give way to forests, with hardscrabble farms wedged in where the terrain allows, much smaller than the valley-bottom spreads just a few miles to the west. The effect is much more traditionally Vermont, a marked contrast after miles and miles of the wide open spaces. State 74 winds its way over the ridge from farmhouse to farmhouse. You'll see a particularly handsome homestead perched on the east side of the ridge overlooking Quiet Valley near Cornwall. A tiny family cemetery, white clapboard barn with slate roof and cupola, and rambling farmhouse command expansive vistas east to the Green Mountains, which crop up into view here. Descending from the ridge, the farmland opens up again near the Lemon Fair

River. You'll pass one more ridge and one last expanse of open land before State 74 takes you into Cornwall and the foothills of the Green Mountains.

State 74 ends in tiny Cornwall, which amounts to little more than a church, a cemetery, and a veterans' monument. State 30 follows a ridge north, offering good views both east and west. This close to Middlebury, the country homes are well kept, many of them the residences of Middlebury College faculty and staff.

You'll start to see craft shops, a sure sign that you're returning to traditional tourist turf. Watch for Cider Hill Road, a straight-ahead left turn about a mile from downtown Cornwall. It takes you past orchards, an abandoned farmhouse, and a tiny one-room school that has been turned into a house. After two miles you'll cross State 125, which links Middlebury and Chimney Point, then it's another two miles into Weybridge Hill, a four-corners with a monument to Silas Wright, a nineteenth-century U.S. senator and general whose questionable claim to fame was that he turned down the vice-presidential nomination.

In Weybridge Hill make two quick turns: right onto State 23, and then immediately left, just after the church, onto Hamilton Road. A dirt road takes you past the Hamilton Farm, with its windmill, and out to the Morgan Horse Farm, where the University of Vermont breeds and trains specimens of the state's equestrian pride and joy. Be sure to take a tour of the farm if you fancy horses. But be careful, the beautiful and spirited Morgans will win your heart.

Then head back to Weybridge Hill and continue north on Quaker Hill Road for a pleasant drive along Otter Creek to State 17. Turning west on State 17, you'll quickly descend back into the Champlain Valley.

At the junction of State 22A and State 17, Addison offers a rare treat for wildlife lovers. The Dead Creek Wildlife Management Area, located a couple of miles west of the intersection, is a migratory crossroads for thousands of Canada and snow geese. The arrivals and departures of enormous flocks of the snow geese are especially dramatic. For a couple of weeks each October, thousands upon thousands of the waterfowl virtually blanket the area, filling the air with the sounds of their honking and complaining while they rest up for the resumption of their flight south. When the snow geese are ready to continue south, huge flocks will suddenly explode out of the marshes, blotting out the sky with clouds of white.

Needless to say, the area is popular with hunters, who are more interested in the Canada geese than they are in the more plentiful snow geese. But hunting is carefully controlled in the best interests of both species.

Though it is especially appealing during migration season, the Dead Creek area is inviting year-round. Take the time to explore the area, with its reedy swamps and oak groves, then head back to State 22A for the quick jaunt back into Vergennes. It's six pleasant miles of farmland—especially good for viewing the sunset over the Adirondacks. You'll be back in Vergennes in time for supper.

In the Area

All phone numbers are in area code 802.

Kennedy Brothers Factory Marketplace, Vergennes, 877-2975

Rokeby Museum, Ferrisburgh, 877-3406

Vermont Pasta Restaurant and Bar, Ferrisburgh, 877-3413

Main Street Bistro, Vergennes, 877-3288

Basin Harbor Club, Vergennes, 475-2311

Lake Champlain Maritime Museum, Vergennes, 474-2311

Addison County Chamber of Commerce, 388-7951

Museum of Native American and French Heritage,
Chimney Point, 759-2412

Morgan Horse Farm, Weybridge, 388-2011

6 ~

The Burlington Area

From Montreal (two hours) take Trans-Canada Highway 10 east to State 133 south; at the U.S. border, State 133 becomes I-89 south to Burlington. From Boston (3 ½ hours) take I-93 north to Concord, New Hampshire, then I-89 north to Burlington. This trip begins and ends in Burlington.

Highlights: *Vermont's largest city, Lake Champlain and mountains, farmlands, Morgans, Huntington Gorge; Shelburne Farms and Museum, Green Mountain Nature Center and Birds of Vermont Museum.*

The Route

US 7 south to Shelburne village, then Harbor Road to Shelburne Farms. Back on US 7, continue south past Shelburne Museum, then turn west on Bostwick Road to Charlotte. In Charlotte village, go east for half a mile back to US 7, then south two miles to the Mount Philo turnoff. From Mount Philo, south one mile to North Ferrisburgh Road, then east through North Ferrisburgh village to Monkton Boro, Monkton Ridge, and Rockville. In Rockville, go south on State 116 to State 17, then east on State 17 for seven miles to Huntington Road. Drive north on Huntington Road to Dugway Road (an unmarked dirt road three miles north of Huntington). Take Dugway Road north to Cochran Road in Richmond. Take Cochran Road west past Richmond town green. Bear right, continuing west, one-half mile past Richmond green (follow signs to Hinesburg). Continue through Fays Corner. In Rhode Island Corners, go right on Pond Brook Road to Mechanicsville. Bear right and continue five miles to the four-way intersection (look for a red brick farmhouse). Turn left (west) and continue one mile to Spear Street Extension. Turn right on Spear Street Extension and continue north back to Burlington. This trip is about seventy-five miles long and takes at least 2 1/2 hours without stops.

Using Burlington, a town worth exploring, as our base, this route rambles through the countryside just south of Vermont's lone city. We'll never be more than half an hour's drive away from the heart of downtown, but you won't find any suburbs. These are country roads.

You've been in Vermont too long when Burlington starts to look like a big city. Vermont's largest city lies where the Winooski River spills into the broadest part of Lake Champlain. Greater Burlington, population 100,000, includes four or five of the state's most densely populated towns and with them a touch of suburbia. Sure, there are shopping malls (only two: residents fought off a third) and strip development (hardly runaway), but for the most part Burlington is a semi-urban island in a sea of near wilderness.

To the west, Lake Champlain stretches to New York state, where the jagged Adirondack Mountains serrate the western sky—a sight to behold at sunset. To the East, Mount Mansfield and Camels Hump, the more often than not snow-clad kings of the Green Mountain range, loom against the clean blue Vermont sky.

If you're still not convinced that there's countryside out there, take a drive in any direction: ten minutes north, south, or east and you're back in farm country viewing dirt roads, barbed-wire fences, and open fields—the land that strip development forgot.

From Burlington, head south for a few miles on US 7 until you see the sign for Bay Road on the right, which leads to the gates of Shelburne Farms. It is a grand estate amassed in the late 1800s by railroad baron William Seward Webb and Lila Vanderbilt Webb. Now whittled down to 1,000 acres, the lakeside parcel was once 4,000 acres.

The Webbs had the best of everything for their country home: They hired Frederick Law Olmsted, also the designer of Central Park, to landscape the still exquisite rolling grounds.

Today the estate operates as a posh inn, Shelburne House, and an experimental farm. The 110-room Queen Anne–style mansion, open summers only, has been restored impeccably and offers stunning lake and garden views. For

Try a sleigh ride at the Shelburne Museum

those who can't afford to stay, come for breakfast and sneak in a tour. Dinner is also served to the public. Tours of the property are available, and a gift shop sells the farm's famous cheddar cheese and other tasty picnic fare. In summer, Shelburne Farms hosts concerts, equestrian events, and art and food festivals.

After a tour of the farm, return to US 7 and drive a few miles farther to the signs on the right for the Shelburne Museum. Don't expect a musty old gallery. Instead, the "museum" is a 100-acre park complex with thirty-five early American buildings: taverns, barns, blacksmith shop, and general store.

Inside, the structures house a fine collection of eighteenth- and nineteenth-century furniture, crafts, and art. Feast your eyes on the quilts, hatboxes, antique clothing, farm tools, weather vanes, and cigar-shop Indians. Transportation buffs will enjoy the 1915 steam locomotive and the SS *Ticonderoga*, a side-wheeler that once plied Lake Champlain.

The museum was founded after 1947 by the late Electra Havemeyer Webb and her husband, J. Watson Webb. While her peers collected art by the great European masters, Mrs. Webb's passion was for things American, things useful. Many of her acquisitions might have seemed ordinary in the first part of this century, but now they make up one of the nation's best collections of folk art and Americana.

From the museum head south again on US 7, watching for a quick right on Bostwick Road. It will lead you into Charlotte, pronounced the Quebec way with the emphasis on the second syllable. Follow the road as it veers south, cutting through farmland and eventually climbing up a ridge, allowing for lovely views of Lake Champlain to the west. Although many Burlington commuters live in these parts the terrain is surprisingly undeveloped. Horses roam in their paddocks, cows meander, and feed corn grows high and green in the summer.

Horsford's Nursery, indicated with a sign on the left, is a fine place to get out for a walk and ogle whatever's in season. Or continue on the road and simply watch for a lovely field of wildflowers on the right shortly before the village of Charlotte. The phlox, Queen Anne's lace, and daisies are so pretty that more than one passerby has been tempted to take the view home. Hence the politely lettered signs not to pick the flowers.

Turn left at the intersection of Charlotte village and head over to US 7. Turn right and head south. Two miles down watch for a left-hand turn, which heads east to Mount Philo, a peak that offers fine views of the lake and Chittenden County. It is open to cars in the summer and walkers year-round. On foot, the walk is steep and strenuous but mercifully short—under forty-five minutes. Picnic tables, telescopes, and rocky lookouts await you at the top of the 930-foot summit. You won't find a better view of the lake and the Adirondacks.

Continue south from Mount Philo and you'll begin to pick up views to the east and the west as the mountain fades. Watch for the first good views of Camels Hump, which will be an old friend by the end of this drive.

About a mile and a half from Mount Philo, turn left on North Ferrisburgh Road and head east out of the valley. You soon enter North Ferrisburgh, part of the greater township of Ferrisburgh, which, until recently, couldn't decide how to spell its own name. Townsfolk struggled with the issue of whether the name of their town should indeed end with an *h*. The debate pitted post office against town clerk, businesses against residents, until it was arbitrated that the spelling should include the controversial *h*. Local signage has been slow to catch up with the decision, and you'll see signs of this schizophrenia, so to speak. Moreover, some residents maintain they won't be told how to spell the name of their own town: They didn't need an *h* before, and they don't need one now.

North Ferrisburgh is a picturesque cluster of houses with a municipal building or two and a bridge over Lewis Creek. Climbing out of town into the open countryside, you'll soon come to a magnificent farm property that appears still to be working, though it has fallen into grave disrepair. The farmyard shows signs of life, but the farmhouse itself, an enormous mansard-roofed affair with exquisite moldings and commanding views, stands sadly neglected.

Continuing west, farmland gives way to groves of pine intermingled with swamp and ledge. The road turns to dirt for a stretch. Here, where the land is unsuitable for farming, the modern-day residence of choice is the ubiquitous mobile home.

They're not much to look at, especially when compared to the neighboring historic farmhouses, but mobile homes, or "trailers," as they are more commonly called, are something of an icon for the Vermont life-style. They appear in the remotest of areas, proof that in Vermont almost anybody can afford a home with a view.

Rolling on through pleasantly rugged countryside into Monkton Boro, where the local ballfield welcomes you to town, go left at the three-way intersection and drive two miles to Monkton Ridge. En route, you'll see flashes of tiny Cedar Lake through the trees on your left. In Monkton Ridge, a rambling farmhouse stands at the head of a three-way intersection, looking back down the road over the lake and to the west.

Go left at the intersection, then look for an immediate right. You'll roll down off the ridge, with views of Camels Hump to the northeast as you head east. There's more rolling farmland ahead, divided among a handful of small working farms. After three miles, you'll come to a four-way

Bringing in the hay

intersection where the road turns to dirt. Climb a ridge past a windbreak of enormous maple trees, forty or fifty of them in a perfect row, connected with barbed wire and stone wall, and watch around the bend for another handsome but dog-eared working farm.

A mile farther, the road turns back to pavement as you head into Rockville, formerly known as State Prison Hollow. The name, according to unconfirmed local legend, dates back to an era when the hollow's populace included a certain un-savory element, likely candidates for the county jail. The hamlet is clustered around Lewis Creek, and a former mill has been converted into the Millhouse Bed and Breakfast, a pleas-ant establishment on the banks of the rushing creek.

Just after the Millhouse, look for Green Mountain Ceme-tery Road and take a left. It's a short drive up the hill to where past residents of Rockville are interred in a lonely, windswept graveyard bordered by a wrought-iron fence. Take in a few of the fading epitaphs and then get on State 116, known locally as Hinesburg Road, and follow Lewis Creek south into Starksboro.

The drive south is a pleasant valley-bottom cruise with the Green Mountains beginning their ascent in earnest on the left and their foothills on the right. In Starksboro, you'll find an ancient post office, built in 1816 and still operating, and working farms that front right onto the main drag, offering up summer produce, honey, and maple syrup in season.

Six miles south of Starksboro, you'll hit the intersection with State 17 on its way up into Appalachian Gap. Head east on State 17, through the hamlets of South Starksboro and Jerusalem. It's seven miles, all uphill, to the intersection with Huntington Road, a left turn that will take you back north, hard against the spine of the Green Mountains.

In the shadow of the 3,500-foot peaks of Mount Ethan Allen, Mount Ira Allen, and Burnt Rock Mountain, you'll roll into Huntington—or at least that's what the official highway sign beside the road says. A few hundred feet after that sign, however, an indignant resident of the hamlet of Hanksville has posted a large "Welcome to Hanksville" sign, hand-lettered, making it clear that Huntington village proper is still a ways up the road, and if that's where you're headed, you should keep going.

So close to the mountain, there's little fallable land, and most of Huntington amounts to winding roads through rocky terrain beside the Huntington River, with a farm squeezed in here and there as the terrain permits. From Hanksville, it's three miles to Huntington Center, where you can pick up a town road due east into Camels Hump State Park.

Camels Hump, named for its distinctive profile, is one of Vermont's most recognizable peaks, and it fairly dominates the Huntington landscape. Much of the town lies within the state park, where you can hike a variety of trails to the summit above the tree line at 4,083 feet. One of the trails leads to the wreckage of a World War II–era B-52 bomber that crashed on the mountainside during a flight up the Winooski Valley on a wintry night. Trying to stay warm, the pilot had flown too low. Some of the crew members were rescued, but lost limbs to the cold. The wreckage remains today, a grim reminder of the crew's dire overnight stay on the mountainside.

Although now forever linked to the camel, the first white man to set eyes on the curious-looking mountain saw things differently. Explorer Samuel de Champlain called it *Le Lion Couchant,* or the sleeping lion. His more imaginative description, however, did not impress cartographers.

From Huntington follow the Huntington River north. You'll pass the left turn for Sherman Hollow with its Green Mountain Audubon Nature Center and its Birds of Vermont Museum, a must-see for bird lovers and folks who enjoy nature trails. Every Halloween, hundreds of revelers come to the center's eerie and marvelous haunted forest. The staff also puts on fine celebrations of the summer and winter solstices.

Three miles north of Huntington, the river takes a sharp turn to the northeast. Follow it, turning right on unmarked Dugway Road, a scenic dirt lane that is definitely optional in mud season (March and April), when it can become virtually impassable.

The road knifes through heavy forest, leaving Huntington for Richmond and the Winooski River Valley below. With the river for company, you'll pass the picturesque Fairmont Farms, where Morgan horses graze in tiny pastures wedged between stream and mountain. The owners, Dr. and Mrs. Ernest Pacquette, have to contend with a fair amount of automobile traffic in the summer, when swimmers come to cool off in Huntington Gorge.

The beautiful and forbidding Huntington Gorge, beginning just below Fairmont Farms, is a popular spot with swimmers despite its tragic history. People are irresistibly drawn to the river, which has cut a deep path through the forest, rushing swiftly over waterfalls and through rock tunnels. The din of the crashing water drowns out conversation; mist hangs in the forest gloom.

Despite its beauty, the gorge can be deadly, especially when spring runoff transforms it into an angry torrent. Hardly a year goes by when some careless swimmer isn't swept to his death in the pounding waters. In 1992, the state was saddened by the loss of state police diver Gary Gaboury, who died trying to recover the trapped body of a swimmer who had drowned a day earlier. A sign now commemorates his heroism, warning thrill seekers of the peril.

At the bottom of Dugway Road, turn left on Cochran Road and follow the Winooski River at the bottom of the valley. The farmland is no more fertile anywhere in Vermont. Keep a sharp lookout for Cochran Ski Area. There's not much to see from the road—a small sign and a charming old farmhouse with a single ski trail running up out of the backyard. But the story of the Cochran family is a rich slice of Vermont life.

The single trail you see (there are others out of sight) was carved out of the woods in the sixties by patriarch Mickey Cochran, a retired General Electric engineer and ski coach. Mickey put his engineering skills to work and erected a tiny rope tow in the backyard, then taught his children how to ski. Under Mickey's tutelage, the Cochran children became world-class racers. Barbara won a gold in the slalom at the 1972 Winter Olympics in Sapporo, Japan. Brother Bobby, who was ranked fifth in the world in downhill and slalom, narrowly missed gold in the slalom at Sapporo when he didn't make a gate near the finish. At one time, there were four Cochrans on the U.S. Ski Team—quite a feat for tiny Richmond, Vermont.

Today the same slopes the Olympians trained on represent one of Vermont's most family-friendly ski areas, when snow conditions allow. There's a T-bar and a rope tow, and a lift ticket costs about the same as a movie.

A mile after Cochrans', you'll hit a three-way intersection at the Old Round Church in Richmond. The church, listed on the National Register of Historic Places, actually has sixteen sides—and no corners, it is said, for the devil to hide in. Local legend has it that sixteen carpenters contributed a wall apiece for the interdenominational church when it was built in 1812–13. A seventeenth carpenter added the cupola. The tiny green in front features a monument commemorating the skiing exploits of the Cochrans.

When you're ready to move on, explore Richmond if you like, crossing the river and stopping in for a bite at the Daily Bread Bakery and Cafe or visiting Harrington Hams. Then return to the Round Church common and continue west on Cochran Road. About a half mile from the church, look for a right turn up the hill—following signs to Hinesburg—and continue west two miles to Fays Corner. You're within seven miles of downtown Burlington here, but it's still strictly country, and will be for the next ten miles as you cut west toward the lake, just below the city.

Bearing left at Fays Corner, it's two miles to Rhode Island Corners. A right turn there on Pond Brook Road takes you down the hill past a pair of magnificent maples and the south end of Lake Iroquois, with views to the west starting to open up.

Pond Brook Road merges with a paved town road, which takes you to a four-corners in the hamlet of Mechanicsville. Bear right, cross State 116 at a stoplight, and roll through scenic countryside toward Shelburne Falls. Finally you begin to see signs of civilization, though it amounts to little more than some modest residential development here and there.

Four miles from State 116, go left at a four corners guarded by a red brick farmhouse and nine gnarled oaks. Less than a mile later, look for a right onto Spear Street Extension for the straight shot north into town.

If you've timed it right, Spear Street is a spectacular vantage point for sunsets. The road runs high along the ridge overlooking Champlain to the west and the Green Mountains to the east. It's some of Burlington's most coveted real estate, and you'll see why as the sun sinks behind the Adirondacks, setting the surface of the lake on fire.

In the Area

All phone numbers are in area code 802.

Shelburne Farms, Shelburne, 985-8686

Shelburne Museum, Shelburne, 985-3344

Horsford's Nursery, Charlotte, 425-2811

Millhouse Bed and Breakfast, Starksboro, 453-2008

Green Mountain Audubon Nature Center, Huntington, 434-3068

Cochran Ski Area, Richmond, 434-2479

Daily Bread Bakery and Cafe, Richmond, 434-3148

Harrington's, Richmond, 434-3411

7 ~

The Mount Mansfield Loop

From Burlington take I-89 south thirty miles south to exit 10 in Waterbury. The trip begins and ends in Waterbury.

Highlights: *Lots of panoramic mountain views, antiques; skiing, golf; Ben & Jerry's ice cream factory, chain-saw sculpture shop, fly-rod shop, Trapp Family Lodge.*

The Route

From Waterbury, head north on State 100. It's ten miles to the Stowe town line, where you'll turn left on Moscow Road for a short dead-end detour up into Nebraska Valley. Return to State 100, and continue north into Stowe village, then turn left onto State 108 (aka the Mountain Road). Seven miles from Stowe village, turn left on the Toll Road for a dead-end detour to the summit of Mount Mansfield. Return to State 108 and continue north through Smugglers Notch into Jeffersonville, then take Upper Valley Road to Underhill Flats. Take State 15 to Jericho, then Lee River Road to Jericho Center. From Jericho Center, take Browns Trace Road, turning left after one mile on Nashville Road. Take Nashville Road through West Bolton to US 2 in Richmond, then US 2 south to Waterbury. The trip is eighty-five miles long and takes at least 2 1/2 hours without stops.

The mountains are magnificent. This trip gives you a chance to enjoy them from a distance, to drive through Smugglers Notch, and to appreciate them up close. You can also choose an ice cream cone at Ben & Jerry's, pick up some fresh cider or an eight-foot wooden moose, take to the ski slopes on skis in winter or a sled in summer, visit a gristmill or the Trapp Family Lodge.

Visible from just about anywhere in northwestern Vermont, Mount Mansfield is Vermont's highest peak and is stamped indelibly on the state's lore. It is also at the heart of one of the largest misconceptions in the state, centering around the origin of its name. While Mount Mansfield does, from many vantage points, resemble a human face—hence Man's-field—that is not why it is so named. The real reason is far less imaginative. The mountain used to lie within the boundaries of the town of Mansfield, no longer extant, which was simply named for the Connecticut town whence came the first settlers of the area.

Armed with that knowledge, you know something about Mount Mansfield that most Vermonters don't —even folks who live and work in its shadow. Still, the mountain does look like a man's face, and parts of it have been named accordingly: the Nose (the highest summit in Vermont, at 4,393 feet), the Chin, the Forehead, and even the Adam's Apple. Interestingly enough, the native Americans didn't see it that way: They called it *Mozodepowadso*, for "mountain with a head like a moose." Man or moose, it's a majestic mountain, and it's worth exploring from every angle, which this route does.

From Waterbury, strike north up the spine of the Green Mountains. The reward is immediate—panoramic views of the rugged Worcester range a few miles to the east and a chance to visit one of Vermont's must-see tourist attractions, the Ben & Jerry's Homemade Ice Cream factory.

It wasn't long ago that you had to be from Vermont to know about Ben & Jerry's. Ben Cohen and Jerry Greenfield, the state's storied emperors of ice cream, founded their kingdom in the 1970s, selling hand-cranked curds from a cramped corner gas station in downtown Burlington. With down-home marketing and plenty of fresh Vermont milk, the folksy entrepreneurs parlayed their business into one of the niftiest corporate success stories of the 1980s.

The Waterbury factory is the company's headquarters and manufacturing crown jewel. You'll see it perched on a hillside, a small herd of token Holsteins munching grass out front, an astronaut's-eye view of planet Earth spreading across the south gable. Stop in for a tour, which includes free samples of the factory's flavor du jour, or just grab a cone and visit the gift shop. When you've had your fill of Chunky Monkey, Oreo Mint, or Rain Forest Crunch, press on toward Waterbury Center and another Vermont standby: apples.

The Cold Hollow Cider Mill in Waterbury Center takes all the ugly duckling drops no one wanted in the fall and turns them into sweet, cold apple cider. Most days you can watch the process. The presses use thousands of pounds of pressure to separate unsuspecting McIntosh apples from their juice. Bushels of fruit are reduced to three-foot rectangles of pulp, no more than a couple of inches thick. These apple-pulp doormats are used to fatten the local cow population. Sample some free cider, then pick up a jug for the road.

As you leave Waterbury Center, Mount Mansfield checks in on the northwest horizon, looking rather ordinary this far away. More impressive is Mount Hunger, due east, king of the heavily forested Worcester range, rising 3,620 feet. If you aren't in a rush, explore the tiny village of Waterbury Center, little more than a clutch of old houses a short ways east of State 100, then head north along the Worcester range on an unmarked back road. It's mostly a dirt lane, and the feel is strictly country.

If you're in the mood for antiquing, stay on State 100. There's a shop every couple of miles or so where you can poke about among the artifacts of life in early Vermont: farm tools, furniture, quilts, linens, knickknacks, clothing, advertising memorabilia, and more. Bargains are rare in the relatively affluent Stowe area, but it's fun to look, and Vermont still offers the possibility of a real find for true antique scavengers. Visitors in the warm months should check the Thursday edition of the *Burlington Free Press* for auction listings in northern and central Vermont. If you've got the time, such auctions yield the best antique bargains.

Staying on State 100, you're about seven miles from I-89 when you leave Waterbury Center for Stowe proper and stumble onto another State 100 curiosity, the chain-saw sculptor's shop. Just look for the bears, moose, horses, buffalo, and cows. No, you're not home on the range—you're at the Spinning Wheel craft shop, home of the late Milo Marshall, Vermont's original chain-saw Michelangelo. Before he passed away in March of 1992, you were likely to find Marshall at work in his shop, hewing wooden wildlife from hardwood stumps. Fortunately, Marshall—like any great artist—had apprentices, so while the master is gone, the tradition of chain-saw carving lives on. If they're at work, watch the sawdust fly. And if you're of a mind to invest in art, you can purchase their work—but you'd better have a truck and a credit card. An eight-foot moose will cost you about $4,000.

About a half mile farther on—just past the Fly Rod Shop, where anglers can browse among handcrafted rods or try one out on the casting pond—Moscow Road intersects from the west. If you're ready for a detour, it's a pleasant drive through tiny Moscow village, past the sawmill dam, along Miller Brook, and up into Nebraska Valley, where the road peters out against the wall of the mountains just over the range from the Bolton Valley Ski Resort.

Back on State 100, press on northward. A few motels, shops, and the local IGA welcome you to Stowe village, which the locals have taken great pains to preserve despite the big-money pressure of the ski industry. Downtown is still pretty much a one-street affair—somewhat to the annoyance of motorists during high tourist season—with a white clapboard church, a handsome red brick library, and a few restaurants and stores.

After you've explored the village, pick up State 108 north, known as the Mountain Road, at Stowe's only stoplight. You'll cross the Little River, then plunge into ski-industry sprawl in earnest.

Ski shops, bike shops, gift shops, boutiques, motels, hotels, spas, resorts, restaurants, bars—anyplace with hopes of separating visitors from their Visa cards—you'll find it on the Mountain Road. Die-hard shoppers will be delighted; others might find it all a little appalling.

In its defense, the Mountain Road retains a certain charm. This is, after all, the heart of ski country. Stowe is the original eastern ski resort, and some of the local businesses have been here from the start, back in the forties and fifties. Local signage laws are strict—you'll have to look hard for the local McDonald's—so for all its eyesores, the still venerable Mountain Road, with the West Branch River and Stowe's acclaimed recreation path running alongside it, and with its views of the mountain looming dead ahead, ski trails beckoning, deserves a little respect. And any skier who has ever crept up it early on a sunny morning after a February storm is willing to grudge it that.

After Stowe, you'll be heading back out into deep country, so take advantage of the civilization. If you want, you can spend a lot on lunch around here: the Top Notch at Stowe Resort and Spa, popular with celebrities, would be delighted to provide you with a fine dining experience. The locals, however—especially the ski bums—prefer something a little less fancy when they're out for lunch or dinner. Two suggestions: For breakfast or lunch, McCarthy's Restaurant, less than a mile up from the village on the right, serves up tasty basics with a great attitude—it's where the skiers fuel up for a day on the slopes; and for lunch or dinner, the Stowe Away Lodge and Restaurant, about three miles up on the right, puts out a terrific Mexican spread in comfortable surroundings—it's where the skiers unwind after a day on the slopes with beer, billiards, and enchiladas.

You'll also see signs for the renowned Trapp Family Lodge. If there had been a sequel to *The Sound of Music*, it would have been set here, on the Vermont hillside where the Baron and Maria von Trapp brought their brood after World

The Trapp Family Lodge

War II. In winter, the Trapp lodge's cross-country ski trails are fabulous and worth the modest ticket price. Rentals are available in a warming shack near the start of the sixty-mile course, which runs through farmland, forest, and along frozen brooks over the 1,700-acre property. After burning off all those calories, head to the Austrian Tea Room for some strudel, chocolate mousse cake, and piping hot tea, served with a lovely view. The lodge also has a proper dining room in the main building, and in summer, outdoor concerts draw hundreds of classical music lovers for picnic suppers on the hillside. Descendants of the von Trapps still run the lodge.

Other things to do on the Mountain Road: stroll and picnic on the recreation path; play eighteen, or hit a bucket, at the immaculate Stowe Country Club; take a balloon ride, rent a bike, pick up a ski hat at venerable Moriarty's; belly up for a pint of bitter and a sandwich at Pickwick's Pub; or just shop till you drop. But chances are, you won't be able to resist, for long, the call of the mountain up the road.

This is your chance to get up close and personal with the magnificent Mansfield. Seven miles up the Mountain Road from Stowe village, the Toll Road takes you to Mansfield's summit. It's open May through mid-October, weather permitting, for a modest fee. Foot traffic, for the truly hardy, is free. The road is a four-mile climb up switchbacks to the base of the Nose, at 4,062 feet, where you can look out over two states and Canada on a clear day. There once was a hotel here, called Mansfield House, which was abandoned in 1957 and razed in 1964. In the nineteenth century a tiny village sprang up around the Mansfield House, with even its own post office, which operated for two months each summer. But there's little sign of all that now, and the summit has been allowed to return to its natural state, prized for its rare Arctic tundra ecosystem.

Back on the Mountain Road, it's another mile to the base of the Mount Mansfield Resort, where the mountain soars out of the parking lot at the base of the ski area. If you're a skier, you've arrived at mecca, and you'll be longing for a schuss down the inviting trails above.

Few ski areas in the country lay claim to the kind of tradition Stowe enjoys. Modern-day skiing got its start here in 1937, when the Mount Mansfield Ski Club—still in existence today—erected a rope tow powered by a Cadillac engine at the base of a ski trail carved through the forest by the Civilian Conservation Corps. Season passes were $5. From beartrap bindings and hardwood skis, Stowe has mushroomed into a vast ski resort, rivaled in Vermont only by Killington and Sugarbush.

Just up the road from the Stowe parking lot you'll see the entrance to its little sister, Spruce Peak. In winter, Spruce offers a gentler and sunnier experience than skiing on the big mountain. It serves as the base for the Mount Mansfield Ski Club and is home to the formidable University of Vermont ski program. In summer, you can pay a few dollars and whiz down Spruce Peak's slopes on the alpine slide, a sort of concrete bobsled run. Hand brakes on the sleds let the pilot go as fast or slow as he or she chooses, but beware, aggressive sledders have been known to walk away with "raspberries" where their elbows or knees met with the unyielding concrete.

Beyond Spruce, you're driving on a section of State 108 that is closed in the winter. You'll soon see why keeping it clear would be next to impossible. The grade quickly steepens, and the road narrows as you begin to climb in earnest over the shoulder of the mountain through Smugglers Notch.

This is the Mountain Road at its most dramatic. The road labors upward through deep forest, winding back and forth through the gloom of foliage cover. Here and there you'll begin to see giant boulders littering the sides of the road— massive silent reminders from the Ice Age, still standing guard where the retreating glaciers left them after leveling off the tops of the state's once towering mountain ranges. Occasional mountain streams, clear and very, very cold, hurtle out of the trees on their way to the Winooski River Valley and Lake Champlain, far away.

Throw your car into low gear and press upward on grades that reach 18 percent in places. You'll see areas to pull over and venture into the forest, or picnic beside a mountain stream. Near the top, the road narrows to a single lane as it squeezes through the notch. The mountain rises up sharply on either side, and the road snakes where it must, picking its way through trees and around massive boulders.

Smugglers Notch itself is an enchanting place. You'll see why the smugglers called it home. Its altitude and situation afford a feeling of invisibility and complete safety. The notch got its name during the War of 1812, when a band of typically libertarian Vermonters used it as a base for smuggling supplies north to Canada, where British troops engaged against the U.S. army offered a lucrative market.

The area, part of the town of Cambridge, is popular in summer with hikers and tourists and even the occasional intrepid cyclist. There's plenty of room to park and walk about. Take a short walk on one of the many trails that diverge from the notch, or take advantage of outdoor grills for a mountaintop picnic. When you've had your fill, point your car down the west side of the range toward Jeffersonville.

It's a whole new world over here. Even the weather is different—often sunny on one side, gray and gloomy on the other. More importantly, you've left Stowe and all its trappings behind for a more realistic view of Vermont. It may be only a ten-minute car ride behind you in summer, but by winter, when the road is closed, it might as well be a different country. Deep snow turns the ten-minute trip into an hour-long affair. The only quick way to do it is on skis: Spruce Peak

Ride a gondola even in the summer

and Smugglers Notch ski areas share a common peak, and if you're confident you can talk the lift operators on the other side into letting you back up the mountain, you can sample both sides of the range in a single day.

As you drive down the west side of the range, the views are spectacular. Make sure to cast a glance over your shoulder now and then for magnificent views back up the mountain. Madonna Mountain rises on your right, and you'll soon reach the parking lot at the base of the Smugglers Notch Ski Area, which is surrounded by condominiums.

Pressing on, the terrain levels out, and farms spring back up on either side of the road, taking advantage of the fertile Lamoille River Valley. The cornfields here seem to grow with a special vigor. Straight stalks spring from the ground, reaching lustily skyward on either side of the road. A narrow brook keeps you company as you roll into the village of Jeffersonville—known in these parts simply as "Jeff." The brook powers a working millstone at the Brewster River Gristmill on the outskirts of town, where you can buy freshly ground flours of various grains along with other Vermont products, or just see how gristmills worked back in the days when any Vermont village worth its millpond had a mill where farmers brought their grain. Many towns still have the remains of such operations. Look for small dams at the center of town—often no longer in use—with dilapidated buildings, sometimes refurbished, sometimes falling in, alongside.

In Jeffersonville, you'll come to a three-way intersection where State 108 crosses State 15, the major east-west artery of northern Vermont. Bear left, and after a couple hundred feet you'll see the Smugglers Notch Inn on the left.

If you decide to stop in, a friendly Basset hound named Oliver greets you with boisterous enthusiasm at the door. No need for any prissy little desk bell here: Oliver summons his full-throated baritone to see to it that your presence is announced. When help arrives, he flops back down on the hardwood and resumes his napping.

The inn is a charming structure built 200 years ago to serve weary horseback travelers. You can have lunch or dinner in the dining room, or take a reasonably priced room under the inn's tin roof. Book well in advance, especially for high seasons. There's a pleasant front porch with wicker chairs and a swing for sitting of an evening and watching Jeffersonville go about its business.

From Jeffersonville, you're a short distance from one of Vermont's unsung shopping opportunities. The Johnson

Once, nearly every country town had a gristmill

Woolen Mill, ten miles east in the town of Johnson, is Vermont's undiscovered L. L. Bean. The mill itself is silent now, but fine woolen clothing is still manufactured on the premises and sold in a small outlet store, and if you're looking for the very latest in Vermont fashion, you've come to the right place. The classic red-and-black-checked wool coats have been keeping farmers warm for decades as they go about their winter chores. Throw on a pair of wool pants and you're ready for deer season. Though not inexpensive, the clothing never goes out of style and lasts a lifetime.

If you're ready to press on, prepare for some breathtaking country scenery on a road that's one of northern Vermont's best-kept secrets.

Pleasant Valley, an idyllic kingdom of dairy farms and rocky pastures, nestles hard against the west side of Mount Mansfield. There's only one entrance, so don't miss it. The turnoff is right next to the Smugglers Notch Inn in Jeffersonville, where a little-traveled Upper Valley Road heads up the hill out of town.

After a mile or so, Pleasant Valley reveals its secrets. One can imagine the sense of awe early settlers must have felt when they first happened into the area. Mount Mansfield is barely recognizable this close to its flanks. None of the discerning features are readily apparent. No nose, no chin, no profile: just sheer soaring mass, miles long, lit from the west by low, late afternoon sun, or blanketed with snow that clings to its sides until late spring, when runoff feeds to overflowing the cattle ponds of hardscrabble farms below.

Upper Valley Road winds over the hilly terrain, past pastures dotted with Holsteins thoughtfully chewing their cuds and rusted farm machinery left where it broke down for the last time. Where the terrain is too forbidding for pasture, stands of birch, maple, and beech line the roads, or low marshy swamps stand crowded with cattails and frogs and peepers. Keep an eye peeled for the occasional lonely sugar-house set back in the shadows of a maple stand, waiting silently for those few weeks in March when it will be the center of activity on the farm, steam bellowing from its chimney, only to be forgotten again when the maples have surrendered their sweetness and the farmer turns his thoughts to plowing and planting. You'll pass an ancient stone farmhouse guarded by massive hardwoods. Weathered barns and leaning silos beg busy farmers for attention, and rusting barbed-wire fences stretch along beside tumbledown stone walls, buckled to and fro by whatever it is, as Robert Frost wrote, that doesn't love a wall.

Dirt roads beckon here and there, and you might want to explore them if Pleasant Valley has cast its spell over you. Four miles out of Jeffersonville you'll join Lower Valley Road, which takes you along the valley floor for a seven-mile drive into Underhill Flats. The closeup views of the mountain are exhilarating—you're about as close to it as you can get and still see it. Just before Underhill Center you can take a left and climb up a steep dirt road into Underhill State Park, which offers a few splendid views of the Champlain Valley to the west and access to the web of trails that ascends the west side of the mountain.

When you reach Underhill Center you begin to leave the mountain behind for the time being. It's a pleasant drive west along Browns River into Underhill Flats, where you'll pick up State 15 west for a short jaunt into Jericho. Leave State 15 where it takes a sharp turn in the center of town. It's a hard left onto poorly marked Lee River Road. Look for signs to Jericho Center. Lee River Road is two miles of field, stream, and forest, bringing you to a three-way intersection. Go right—left takes you back to Underhill Flats—and you'll climb a hill into tiny Jericho Center, a charming hamlet that has escaped the urban pressure of Chittenden County.

There's little more to Jericho Center than a town green and a church. The only business is Desso's family-run country store. You'll find a tidy town common with picnic tables and a plaque that pays tribute to one-time resident "Snowflake" Bentley, the first man to capture on film the beauty and individuality of snowflakes.

As you leave Jericho Center, be sure to bear left and stay on Browns Trace Road (*trace* is an archaic word for "path" or "trail"). It's a three-mile drive past farmhouses and newer homes of Burlington commuters to where little-traveled Nashville Road intersects on the left.

Nashville Road turns to dirt and takes you back east toward the mountains. Bolton Mountain soars to 3,680 feet straight ahead, and you'll catch your last glimpses of Mansfield to the north. You've seen it from all sides now—something not many Vermonters can claim.

You'll pass the entrance to West Bolton Golf Club on the right—an inexpensive and out-of-the-way nine-hole course—then the road takes a hard right and heads south down the flanks of the mountains. The road is steep in places and cuts through dark, heavy forest littered with more glacial boulders like those you saw around Smugglers Notch. Where the trees part overhead, you'll catch glimpses of Camels Hump to the south as the road descends toward US 2 in Jonesville at the bottom of the Winooski River Valley.

Jonesville is a tiny town amounting to little more than six or eight buildings wedged between the road, the interstate, and the river. The most remarkable landmark is a World War II–era steel bridge, which carries you across the Winooski on Cochran Road.

If you've had enough for one day, head south on US 2 to Waterbury to complete your ring around Mount Mansfield. The access road to Bolton Valley Ski Area—a well-marked left turn about six miles south of Richmond—is a steep climb up into the mountains. Or, as an alternate to US 2, which travels along the north side of the Winooski River to Waterbury, there's a lonely dirt road that hugs the south bank. It takes a little longer, but it gets you away from the interstate.

In the Area

All phone numbers are in area code 802.

Ben & Jerry's factory, Waterbury, 244-5641

Cold Hollow Cider Mill, Waterbury Center, 244-8771

The Spinning Wheel, Waterbury Center, 244-8883

The Fly Rod Shop, Stowe, 253-7346

McCarthy's Restaurant, Stowe, 253-8626

Stowe Away Lodge and Restaurant, Stowe, 253-7574

Top Notch at Stowe Resort and Spa, Stowe, 253-8585

Trapp Family Lodge, Stowe, 253-8511

Moriarty's Hats and Sweaters, Stowe, 253-4052

Stowe Mountain Resort (gondola rides, alpine slide), Stowe, 253-7311

Brewster River Gristmill, Jeffersonville, 644-2987

Smugglers Notch Inn, Jeffersonville, 644-2412

Smugglers Notch Ski Area, Jeffersonville, 899-4089

Desso's General Store, Jericho Center, 899-3313

West Bolton Golf Club, West Bolton, 434-4321

Bolton Valley Ski-Summer Resort, Bolton, 434-2131

8 ~

Champlain Islands Splendor

From Burlington take I-89 north to exit 17 in Milton. The trip is 115 miles long and takes most of a day.

Highlights: *Sixth largest lake in the country, water views, state parks, wildlife refuge, campgrounds, beaches, maple sugar country; sailboarding, fishing; Grand Isle State Park, Fort St. Anne, Vermont Maple Festival in spring.*

The Route

Go north on U.S. 2 to Alburg Center, with a brief detour on East Shore Road in South Hero. From Alburg Center, take State 78 to Swanton, then US 7 through Saint Albans back to Burlington.

Vermont is best known for its gentle mountains and rural landscapes, but some of its most spectacular scenery is waterfront. The Champlain Islands route, which begins and ends in Burlington, offers a pleasant sampling of lakefront, farmland, wetlands, mountain views, and country villages. You'll discover roadside farm stands and woodsy campgrounds and sample the rich Franco-Canadian tradition that colors much of northern Vermont and its people.

The islands, which, taken together, make up Grand Isle County, are sometimes described as Vermont's Cape Cod, but don't look for crowds, high prices, or Kennedys. Any resemblance to Hyannisport is fleeting at best.

At 109 miles long, Lake Champlain is the sixth largest lake in the country. It is of great historic, economic, and sentimental importance to Vermont. Its shoreline is considered the western frontier of New England, and with connections north to the St. Lawrence Seaway and south to the Hudson River, it is the major intercoastal waterway of the Northeast.

French explorer Samuel de Champlain discovered the lake in 1609. The first white settlers arrived in 1666 at its northern tip, but were forced to abandon their settlement on Isle La Motte due to harsh weather and inhospitable Abenaki Indians.

Historians argue over the exact nature of Native American settlements in the Champlain Basin, but their influence looms large in myth. The Abenaki believe the lake was carved out by Ojihozo, the Creator, who then turned himself into Rock Dunder—an island rock near Shelburne Point—so he could forever enjoy his creation.

Heading north from Burlington you'll notice that I-89 is the beauty queen of interstates—no billboards (they're outlawed in Vermont), no trash (credit the small population and an environmentalist conscience), and lots of rolling green farmland.

The foothills of the Green Mountains rise gently to the east, and Lake Champlain and New York lie to the west. Early in the ten-minute drive on the highway, you'll cross the Winooski River. Look east to where it has carved a deep gorge out of the rocks. Along the way, notice the geological strata left over from construction of the highway. Lake Champlain was formed 13,000 years ago when atmospheric warming caused a gigantic glacier, more than a mile thick, to melt.

Above Lake Champlain

At exit 17 in Milton, turn right onto US 2, gateway to the Champlain Islands. Sailboarders flock to the islands when the wind is up, and cyclists enjoy the winding country roads and flat terrain. Fishing is popular summer and winter—ice-fishing huts dot the lake by January—and the sunsets are stunning year-round.

It's four miles from the highway to Sand Bar State Park and the first good views of Lake Champlain. Along the way you'll cross the Lamoille River, wide and slow as it nears the end of its journey to the lake from deep in the Northeast Kingdom.

The park entrance is on the right, across from a boat access to the Sandbar Wildlife Refuge. The refuge, mostly on the south side of the road, is a sprawling wetlands area popular with fishermen and waterfowl sportsmen.

On the north side of the highway, the state park's beach is mobbed in summer with swimmers, picnickers, and sailboarders, who like the warm shallow water.

The French-Canadian influence is strong in the area, owing to its history and its proximity to Montreal, just over an hour away. In addition to the tourists, many French-Canadians have settled in here, so you'll see some bilingual signs and hear the flat, nasal inflection of Quebec French.

If you're traveling in the off-season, or if it doesn't look like the beach is overly crowded, Sandbar State Park is a nice

Along the lake

place for a quick break. Otherwise, leave the crowds behind and head over the mile-long sandbar bridge, where the town of South Hero welcomes you to Grand Isle.

The scenery improves as you leave the mainland. The area is still largely given over to dairy farming and orchards. Hay, corn, and pasture take up most of the gently rolling terrain. The highway is punctuated by the occasional lonely survivor from the days before Dutch elm disease, when elm trees canopied many a Vermont lane.

You can stop for supplies at the Grand Isle Store, a small country store about eight miles north of the sandbar, where tourists and locals browse the aisles on creaky maple floorboards. The high ceiling is pressed tin. A pot-bellied stove—forgotten in summer—stands guard in the corner, awaiting winter, when Arctic air blasts the unprotected landscape from the north. The store has a butcher's counter and a fair supply of fresh vegetables in season. You'll find postcards, video rentals, lottery tickets, milk, beverages, and staples.

Fill up your tank and you're off again. For a better view of the shoreline, leave US 2 and take East Shore Road—it's a right turn directly across the street from the Grand Isle Store. You'll roll down a country lane through cornfields toward the water, where the road turns to dirt and arcs north, hugging hard by the shore and offering access to the lake.

Don't look for beaches here. The shoreline is typical of the area: rocky and inhospitable to bare feet. Kids in these parts learn to swim with their sneakers on. Still, you'll manage to find a spot where you can dabble your feet and share a sandwich and a thermos of coffee.

East Shore Road meanders in and out of forests and fields along the shore, affording splendid views across the water to the mainland. You'll pass Grand Isle State Park, which has all the amenities if you're looking for a place to camp.

After about five miles, the road turns to pavement again and you'll come to a vaguely marked intersection. Turn right to stay on East Shore Road North. The road turns back to dirt, and you'll immediately pass the Pomykala Produce Farm. Stop in for fresh vegetables and flowers in season, or continue north along the shore for more good views across the water.

While you're taking in those views, remember to keep an eye skyward for birds and fowl. Lake Champlain is a crowded migratory route for many species. You'll see mostly red-tailed hawks soaring on island thermals, but bald eagles are on the comeback, so be alert.

East Shore Road rejoins US 2 just before it leaves Grand Isle for the island of North Hero. A drawbridge links the two, and Knight Point State Park, a day-use park, welcomes you to North Hero. The park is open daily from 10:00 A.M. to sunset for a modest admission fee. It offers nature trails, volleyball courts, picnic tables, a sandy beach, horseshoe pits, and boat rentals.

A mile farther, you'll see the sprawling lawns of the lakeside Shore Acres Inn and Restaurant. A shop sells Adirondack chairs, quilts, crafts, etc.—none of them antique—and the hotel keeps a set of golf clubs on hand for guests who want to put those acres and acres of lawn to use. The hotel is situated a couple hundred feet from the water on a gentle slope. There's a dock for those inclined to do a little fishing, or guests can simply relax in Adirondack chairs situated along the porch and at strategic points about the property, perfect for taking in sunrises. Rates are reasonable. Book well in advance.

A little farther north you'll roll into the village of North Hero, with its tidy public library, charming church, and sturdy little houses made of brick and stone, solid enough to have withstood island gales down through the years. You can dine or stay for the night at North Hero House, which has rooms right on the water, overlooking a snug harbor. A nearby stone church has lovely stained glass windows and a sign in the parking lot bearing North Hero's version of the Eleventh Commandment: "Thou Shalt Not Park Here." Violators, one presumes, risk more than a parking ticket.

If you're ready for lunch or a light dinner, you're in for a treat at Birdland, a campy roadside burger restaurant just a few miles north of North Hero. The circa 1950 tableware and nautical bric-a-brac speak of bygone days and summers by the shore. Sit at the counter, or in the screened-in back porch, where lake views and gentle breezes drift through a homey array of wind chimes. The one-page menu offers "hamburgs," delectable milk shakes, and all the diner basics. The priciest item is a $3.95 fried clam and french fry plate. Birdland is open from June to Labor Day.

Continue on US 2 north through South Alburg. After about seven miles, you'll cross the bridge onto the Alburg peninsula and turn west onto State 129 toward Isle La Motte.

The three-mile drive across the peninsula runs past shore and marshland, as well as the Alburg Country Club, which has an eighteen-hole public golf course with views of the lake. Greens fees are $17 during the week and $24 on weekends.

A few hundred yards after the country club, State 129 veers left and crosses a short land bridge to Isle La Motte, the remotest of the Champlain Islands. It's less than a mile to the right-hand turn for St. Anne's Shrine.

History buffs will enjoy a visit to Fort St. Anne. The Roman Catholic shrine, open from May 15 to October 15, marks the site of Vermont's first white settlement, founded in 1666, where Vermont's first Roman Catholic Mass was celebrated.

Harsh weather and unfriendly Indians drove the French settlers off after a winter, despite their prayers to patron St. Anne of Lourdes, Jesus' grandmother. In the 1890s, the

Bishop of Burlington reclaimed the site as a holy place. It was run first by the Jesuits and is now run by the Edmundite brothers.

French-Canadians flock here, especially on feast days when open air Mass is celebrated. Weddings and baptisms are also performed in the outdoor chapel. Many families progress to the sandy beach and picnic tables to continue the festivities.

People pray at several spots about the grounds, including a gold-leaf statue to Anne of Lourdes that was rescued from the Cathedral of the Immaculate Conception in Burlington. Fire destroyed most of the church in 1972, sparing little more than the statue that stood atop it. The statue languished in storage for nineteen years, and was brought to the shrine in 1991. The gift shop sells religious souvenirs, including medallions for all the saints. The priests offer blessings for free.

From the shrine, take State 129 back to the peninsula and turn north toward Alburg. Old family farms and more sturdy stone houses guard the road, commanding views across the water to New York.

In Alburg, make time for two stops. The Alburgh Country Store—some locals favor the *h* spelling—is an enterprising combination of soda fountain and antique shop. The dried flower arrangements are beautiful, and the basement is cluttered with crocks, furniture, glassware, and old prints. The quilts (new) run from $120 to $240.

If you're there on a Saturday, ask the folks at the counter about the Alburg Auction House, a quirky slice of island life. Every week in summer, the auction runs from 2:00 P.M. to 6:00 P.M. and 7:00 P.M. to midnight in a warehouse a few blocks southwest of the store.

Real antique treasures are few and far between at the auction, but the merchandise turns over weekly. Patrons sit in old movie-theater chairs, casting dubious eyes over huge piles of cast-off merchandise crammed to the rafters, while auctioneers gently prod and cajole bargain hunters into buying. The cigarette smoke gets pretty bad, even in the "no-smoking" section, but brave souls linger in hopes of scoring the occasional bargain, such as fifteen-dollar mission-style oak chairs.

From Alburg, head for Swanton via Vermont 78. The terrain is flat and a little dull as you drive east over the peninsula. In August, the fields are crowded with five-foot spikes of purple loosestrife, a handsome wildflower brought to North America by homesick European settlers. Unchecked by any natural predators on this side of the Atlantic, it has become something of a handsome nuisance, choking out indigenous vegetation.

After about five miles you'll emerge on the east side of the peninsula, where a long, low drawbridge takes you across the mile-wide Missisquoi Bay back to the Vermont mainland, where the Missisquoi Wildlife Refuge sprawls over 6,000 acres of Missisquoi River delta. Birders, especially, will want to make time to stop here. Great flocks of migratory birds take advantage of the protected river, lakeshore, and wetlands—both natural and managed—for breeding, feeding, and resting on their Atlantic flyway journeys. The array of ducks is dazzling, especially in fall: ringnecks, teal, blacks, woods, goldeneyes, mergansers, and mallards glide glassy-eyed over the dark, quiet waters among wild rice and cattails. The crown jewel of the refuge is the Shad Island great blue heron rookery, a sight to behold in nesting season, when mates set up shop in enormous nests and tend their hungry broods. The refuge is also home to a plentiful population of frogs. In fact, they are so plentiful in the fields along the river that licensed hunters are allowed to harvest them for food.

You've heard of deer season; frog season runs from July 15 to September 30.

Continuing east, the road into Swanton is bordered on the right by the Central Vermont Railroad and on the left by the Missisquoi River. The river is wide and slow, flanked by hayfields and towering trees.

Swanton village presents its homely side first. The north end of town is marred by some unfortunate commercial architecture, but do not fear, the view rapidly gives way to pleasant, older brick municipal structures clustered around a tidy village green, home in the summer to a pair of royal swans. You'll leave town on a treed residential promenade lined with stately homes from another, more prosperous era, when the Robin Hood-Remington Arms factory, now long abandoned, fueled a robust local economy with jobs making arms for World War I.

In fact, with its pleasant tinge of decaying grandeur, Swanton serves as a fitting preview to northwest Vermont's crown city, Saint Albans. The convergence of the Lake Champlain shipping routes and the railroads once blessed this area with considerable wealth, and Saint Albans was the hub. Railroad magnates made, squandered, and remade great fortunes in the late nineteenth and early twentieth centuries, and genteel residential areas, still proud, if a bit frayed around the edges, bear testimony to their wealth.

Approaching town from the north, you get a fitting preview of what's ahead. Look for a mobile-home park on the right, and immediately after you'll see its unlikely neighbor, an immense stone mansion with crumbling carriage house perched on a rise amid deep forest and landscaped grounds.

Such residential architecture is Saint Albans's most remarkable facet. When you get to town, take a drive through its hillside neighborhoods and pick out your favorite house.

There are magnificent examples to choose from in almost every style, many of them lovingly restored as the city has come more recently onto better times.

Downtown is centered around Taylor Park, a sloped green with gazebo and water fountain, fronted on the west by Main Street and busy commercial blocks, and on the east by a stately row of churches and municipal buildings. You can forage in the Main Street shops for an afternoon snack, or visit the Franklin County Museum with its period rooms and exhibits. A plaque on the green bears testimony to Saint Albans's brush with Civil War fame, when a party of Confederate raiders infiltrated from Canada, robbed a bank, killed a man, and made off with 201,000 Union dollars.

If you're in town in April, don't miss the incomparable Vermont Maple Festival. The locals turn out in force to stage a weekend extravaganza of lumberjack contests, bake-offs, sugar-on-snow parties, and the crowning of the Vermont Maple King and Queen. The ubiquitous local delicacy is sugar on snow, a dubious combination of hot syrup on snow, often served with a side of pickles and doughnuts.

For an up-close look at sugaring—a cornerstone of the Vermont agricultural economy—visit the H. J. Howrigan & Sons Farm in nearby Fairfield, where they still do it the old-fashioned way, with horses, buckets, wood-fired evaporators, and plenty of manpower. Using more modern techniques, Vermont has become the leading producer of maple syrup in the country with an average annual yield of 500,000 gallons. The season runs from late February in the south to April in the north.

By now you'll be ready to head back to Burlington and call it a day. Leaving town on US 7, the sunsets over Lake Champlain can be spectacular. It's a pleasant drive through farm country to the tiny town of Georgia, where you can pick up I-89 for the short hop back to Burlington.

Heading back to the sugarhouse

In the Area

All phone numbers are in area code 802.

Grand Isle Store, South Hero, 372-4771

Grand Isle State Park, South Hero, 372-4300

Pomykala Produce Farm, Grand Isle, 372-5157

Knight Point State Park, North Hero, 372-8389

Shore Acres Inn and Restaurant, North Hero, 372-8722

North Hero House, North Hero, 372-8237

Birdland Restaurant, North Hero, 372-4220

Alburg Country Club, Alburg, 796-3586

St. Anne's Shrine, Isle La Motte, 928-3362

Alburg Auction House, Alburg, 796-3572

Alburgh Country Store, Alburg, 796-3417

H. J. Howrigan & Sons Farm, Fairfield, 827-4479

Vermont Maple Festival Council, Saint Albans, 524-5800

9 ~

The

Kingdom

From Burlington take I-89 south thirty-five miles to exit 8 in Montpelier. From there take US 2 seven miles to State 14 and drive twenty-two miles to Hardwick. The trip begins and ends in Hardwick.

Highlights: *Stirring views, abundant lakes, rugged countryside, state forest; fishing and other outdoor recreation; Bread & Puppet Theater Museum, Orleans County Fair in August, Old Stone House Museum.*

The Route

From Hardwick take State 15 to State 16 north heading for Greensboro Bend. Stay on State 16 through Barton to Westmore and Lake Willoughby. From there take State 5A to State 58 through Orleans and Irasburg. Go east on State 58 to State 14. Turn left off State 14 to Craftsbury Common, East Craftsbury, and Greensboro. Go south to Hardwick to complete the loop. The ninety-mile trip takes at least 2 ½ hours without stops.

Like a handsome farm girl in an old dress who is over-looked at the Saturday night dance, the Northeast Kingdom is often passed over by tourists. Nonetheless, it promises some of the most stirring views in the state.

It is a kingdom of untracked mountains, clear, cool lakes, and rugged countryside that for the most part remains undeveloped. Logging, dairy farming, and small businesses are still the way of life. The scenery is spellbinding: Lake Willoughby, a fjordlike finger of water guarded by sheer cliffs on either side; Craftsbury Common, with its classic New England green surrounded by trim white clapboard houses; and the surreal hayloft of the Bread & Puppet Theater Museum.

Hardwick, by today's standards, is a blink-or-miss-it town of approximately 2,700 people. It has a friendly bookstore, The Galaxy, a few good restaurants, and the requisite volunteer fire department, town hall, and white steepled churches.

Today the rattle and roar of trucks loaded with logs is the most industrious sign about, but Hardwick was once a major granite processing center. The granite came by rail from quarries in Woodbury, five miles to the south, and was milled along the banks of the Lamoille River. From the 1870s to the 1920s, the mills attracted thousands of skilled European artisans to a hard life in the sheds.

Heading out of Hardwick on State 15, take a left onto State 16 toward Glover. This road is nostalgic for many Vermonters who spent summers at "camps," or unheated cottages, on the abundant lakes and ponds scattered through the skull-shaped piece of land between State 16 and State 14 to the west.

The road is narrow but in good shape, with views of family farms that are still in operation, pine-lined ridges, and small country towns, many of them frayed and threadbare, but still proud.

Greensboro Bend, one of the first towns on the way, is quiet and gritty, with a lonesome 1872 train station that's worth a look for its handsome stick-style architectural detail.

The scenery along State 16 is beautiful all year. In late autumn, watch for the spectacular yellow pointed tops of the tamarack trees. Before the snow flies, the countryside is sepia-toned and subdued, beautiful in a lonely, hushed way. Snow changes everything, spreading a cozy white blanket over the chilly countryside. In spring, runoff turns the region's web of dirt roads to ribbons of muck, impassable to all but the stoutest of vehicles. By summer, lush growth softens the landscape beneath the deep clear blue of Vermont skies, and Holsteins graze in impossibly green pastures sprinkled with yellow dandelions.

There are still many active farms along this route, holdouts in Vermont's declining dairy industry. Dairy farms' numbers fell from 11,153 in 1950 to 2,265 in 1993, and today Vermont's mostly Holstein cows produce 2.3 billion pounds of milk annually.

A farm in the Northeast Kingdom

Enamel blue Harvestore silos shine brightly in the sun and the pastures are lumpy and muddy from heavy cow traffic. Clapboard is the building material of choice, and you'll notice that many farmhouses are connected to their barns, saving farmers a walk though heavy snow in winter.

Continue on curving State 16, past lakes and swamps. Pass lonely little Horse Pond and, a few miles farther, watch for a lonely plaque beside the road marking Runaway Pond.

Now nothing more than a boggy soup of cattails and brush, there was once a lake here known as Long Pond. In 1810, the lake "ran away" when locals tried to channel water out of it to power nearby mills. The ditchdiggers hit quicksand and the lake broke free. It took six hours to drain, sending a wall of water, sometimes as high as fifty feet, toward Lake Memphremagog twenty miles to the north. Houses and forest were destroyed in its path. To this day you can see signs of the flood. A short distance farther, watch for a left-hand turn to Shadow Lake. If you're looking for a spot to picnic or swim, turn left here and drive a mile to the Shadow Lake public beach. It's small and sandy, with nice views of the cottage-lined lake and the steep mountains that surround it.

Back on State 16, head north for a few miles to the junction with State 122. You'll see it just before an old country cemetery with bleached white headstones.

About a mile up State 122, watch for a crudely painted sign announcing the Bread & Puppet Theater Museum, housed in a ramshackle barn. Don't let the humble appearance fool you: Every summer thousands of people come to this otherwise sleepy site to see one of Vermont's most bizarre theatrical spectacles. In the natural amphitheater just south of the museum, a massive outdoor pageant known as Our Domestic Resurrection Circus takes place every summer, with dates varying each year.

The circus and its parent, Bread & Puppet Theater, are the creative brainchildren of Peter Schumann, who founded the theater in 1962 on New York's Lower East Side. From the beginning, the exaggerated, crudely fashioned puppets were political and populist, protesting rents, rats, and other problems in the neighborhood, and later leading hundreds of people in street protests of the Vietnam War.

Schumann and his wife, Elka, brought the theater to Vermont in 1970. Although it has toured the world, Bread & Puppet's best-known production is its annual summer circus. Visitors from throughout New England camp out in neighboring fields, coming out of their tents Saturday to mill through the sideshows and skits that are performed all day leading up to the circus and to sample the coarse breads and tangy garlic mayonnaise that are served free in the meadow. Then the audience settles down on blankets for the moment when the circus begins with a cacophony of drums and horns. A wildly painted school bus barrels down a hill, banners are unfurled, enormous "puppets" stagger about on stilts, and the volunteer cast dances and sings.

If you miss the circus, be sure and stop into the museum, where the puppets, banners, and other odds and ends from past performances are displayed. It's open from May to October, often unstaffed. Go through self-serve, following the directions to the light switch and donation boxes. (Leave checks, no cash.)

After Bread & Puppet, head back on State 122 to State 16 bound for Barton. You'll descend into tiny Glover, past Currier's general store and the ramshackle Busy Bee restaurant. After Glover, look for the Orleans County Fairgrounds on the outskirts of Barton. The fairground comes to life for a week each August, drawing Kingdom residents to tractor pulls and girlie shows.

Heading into Barton, look for the Barton Academy and Graded School on the right, built in 1907, with its handsome façade of red and ivory brick.

Stay on State 16, which takes a sharp right in the center of town, climbs a hill, then takes a sharp left toward Westmore. As you climb the ridge Crystal Lake spreads below, bordered by sharp cliffs along its northeast shore. The road ascends toward Barton Mountain, elevation 2,235 feet. The views are spectacular as the road gains altitude, finally opening out onto a plateau of farmland. Thin wires of electric fence run parallel to the road, keeping cows and horses in their pastures. Round bales of hay, wrapped in thick white plastic for winter, sit in the fields so as not to take up valuable space in the weathered barns with old tin roofs.

The fields are rocky and rolling. While beautiful to look at, they explain why Vermont evolved as a dairy state and not a crop state. In fact, many of Vermont's early farmers were struck by "western fever" for flat, wide open farmland. By 1870, Vermont had given over half its native-born population to the rest of the country.

About seven miles from Barton look for the first spectacular views of Lake Willoughby slicing through the mountains in a geological wonder that recalls the fjords of Scotland or Norway. Approached from the north end, the five-mile lake stretches down to Willoughby Gap between the base of twin mountains, Mount Pisgah and Mount Hor.

Mount Pisgah, the larger of the two at 2,751 feet, was fittingly named for the place the Lord sent Moses to view the promised land. Both mountains are part of the 7,000-acre Lake Willoughby State Forest. Its hiking trails offer spine-tingling views of both Lake Willoughby and the White Mountains to the east. Camping is allowed.

From the north, you'll drive along the east shore of the lake through Westmore on State 5A. The grand scenery explains why the lake was once called "the Lucerne of America."

In the early 1800s the lake was a stomping ground for hunters and fishermen. By the mid-nineteenth century it blossomed as a summer resort community with steamers, luxury hotels, tearooms, and dance halls. Time and fire have all but erased the grandeur of the past, and today the lake is bordered by state forest and modest cottages.

Setting out along the water on Lake Road, or State 5A, you'll pass small cottages, motels, and the hillside Willoughvale Inn, a replica of its nineteenth-century predecessor. The large dining room features commanding views of the lake.

Lake Road is wedged in between cliff and water for spectacular views. From the car window, the dark band of water seems inches away. Across it on the other side, sheer cliffs plunge into the water, leaving almost no shore. Steamboat captains used to entertain passengers by calling attention to what seemed to be shapes—a cow, a lion's head, a Native American woman—on the cliffs of Mount Pisgah.

The unskeptical populace also spoke of a secret underground passage between Lake Willoughby and its geological peer, Crystal Lake. Items lost in one lake, they said, occasionally turned up in the other, including in one case, an entire team of oxen that went through the ice on Crystal.

Toward the south end of the lake, hikers and campers find access to the state forest. Otherwise, double back to the north end, passing the boat access where fishermen put in to angle for the lake's well-stocked supply of salmon and rainbow trout.

At the north end, where you came in, head out on State 5A, veering left on State 58 in the direction of Orleans.

If you have time, take a short side trip to the Old Stone House Museum in Brownington. On State 58, pass Evansville and look for a sign to Brownington Center. Turn right to the center, and then left to the charming nineteenth-century village where the Old Stone House, built in the 1830s, is located. The village is listed in the National Register of Historic Places, and has about it a musty, undisturbed quality.

The main attraction is the oblong, four-story school built by the Reverend Alexander Twilight, who is believed to be America's first black college graduate and first black legislator. With the help of his neighbors, Twilight split and hauled granite blocks to build the school where he would spend the next two decades teaching the basics to children from miles around. The thirty-room school is now a museum displaying tools, crafts, kitchenware, furniture, and art from the region's past. In summer the village boasts several lovely gardens. The museum is open from May 15 to October 15.

From Brownington head south onto State 58, and in minutes the town of Orleans comes into view. Elegant hilltop mansions look down on the sleepy main street. The town's major employer is an Ethan Allen furniture factory.

From Orleans, follow the signs on State 58 to Irasburg. It's quaint but not overly so, with a village square lined by church, library, and two general stores. In summer, the locals play softball on the diamond in the green.

In Irasburg pick up State 14 and head south, through more farmland. This section of Vermont has a very remote feel and tourists are few. The Black River weaves along the road, and the occasional abandoned farmhouse—roof sagging and windows boarded up—sits neglected on the edge of a field.

In Albany, more than one big old Victorian house has seen better days. The packrat mentality is evident in junk-cluttered wraparound porches.

Shortly beyond Albany, look for a left-hand turn and a sign that directs drivers to nearby Craftsbury. If you miss this turnoff don't panic, there's another one a few miles down State 14.

The first turnoff runs through cornfield and pasture, past farmhouse and rustic cabin. As the road climbs the hill toward Craftsbury, the forest thickens. On the left side note the small plastic hoses attached to maple trees. The sap runs into hoses and to a central collection point.

Craftsbury is actually a composite of scattered hamlets strewn over Currier & Ives countryside. Much of it is located on a plateau, with views of farmland stretching out on either side, and clouds hovering just overhead, as if heaven were right upstairs.

This is not the kind of town where clothes are hung out to dry. Signs of genteel wealth are visible in the immaculately groomed lawns, freshly painted homes, and the occasional Range Rover parked in the driveway.

At the top of the hill, turn right toward Craftsbury Common, the pride of the neighborhood. White clapboard pervades, as if by unwritten law. The Inn on the Common is one of the poshest places to dine and sleep in the Northeast Kingdom. It's known for lovely gardens, clay tennis courts, a fine wine cellar, and great views.

Craftsbury Common was founded by a Massachusetts pub owner in the mid-1700s who came to Vermont fleeing his debts. Despite his financial difficulties, he was able to convince 150 of his Sturbridge, Massachusetts, neighbors to join him in Craftsbury.

The Craftsbury Center, located 2 1/2 miles from the common in an old boarding school, is one of the most popular attractions in town, especially for the outdoorsy crowd. Open nine months of the year, the full-service inn draws 4,000 visitors annually, many of them sports lovers who canoe, row, mountain bike, and orienteer in the summer. In winter, cross-country skiers revel in the center's 105 kilometers of trails. Craftsbury is considered something of a snow belt: often it has plenty of cover when other places in Vermont don't.

From the common, head down the hill into the town of Craftsbury. New Englanders do have a funny way of organizing their communities, with towns, villages, and commons forming sets and subsets.

The town is a bit less precious than the common, with a couple of vintage churches, gas stations, and a store. Head south out of town and look for the signs to East Craftsbury, yet another limb in this tree of hamlets. Of all the drives on this route, this leg is perhaps the most beautiful, especially in winter.

The narrow road winds up over a ridge, past gorgeous old farmhouses, often running parallel to sturdy stone walls. The snow collects on the apple trees and the woods brim with Christmasy evergreens. It's a magical setting. In East Craftsbury, visit the John Woodruff Memorial Library, a general store built in the 1840s that has since been converted into a trove for books.

Continue south toward Greensboro. After a few miles, watch for the Highland Lodge on a hillside to the left of the road. The Victorian lodge and cabins are clean and quaint. The hearty meals are excellent and recreation is abundant: tennis, hiking, boating, and swimming on Caspian Lake in the summer; cross-country skiing and skating in the winter.

Caspian comes into view around Highland Lodge and can be glimpsed through the trees on the way to Greensboro. The hourglass-shaped lake is ringed by mountains and is generally considered to be one of the most beautiful bodies of water in Vermont.

Greensboro is a historic resort community where writers, socialites, and nature lovers have summered for more than a century. The locals refer to the summer colony as Deansboro, because so many of the first summer residents were college deans and professors.

For a better view of the lake, go into Greensboro and take a right at the sign for the public beach. There are picnic tables, a boat access, and a wooded path that runs along the shore.

The hub of this genteel town is Willey's Store, a rambling two-story affair that is crammed full of groceries, clothing, and hardwares. Sandwiches are sold at a deli counter.

From Greensboro, head southwest out of town on the road to East Hardwick to complete the loop.

In the Area

All phone numbers are in area code 802.

Bread & Puppet Theater, Glover, 525-6972

Willoughvale Inn, Westmore, 525-4123

Old Stone House Museum, Brownington, 754-2022

Inn on the Common, Craftsbury Common, 800-521-2233

Craftsbury Center, Craftsbury Common, 800-729-7751
(Open nine months a year.)

Highland Lodge, Greensboro, 533-2647 (Closed late fall and late spring.)

Willey's Store, Greensboro, 533-2621 and 533-2554

Index

Index

Other titles in the Country Roads Series:

Country Roads of Indiana
Country Roads of Illinois
Country Roads of Michigan
Country Roads of Massachusetts
Country Roads of Kentucky
Country Roads of New Hampshire
Country Roads of Ohio
Country Roads of Pennsylvania
Country Roads of Hawaii
Country Days in New York City
Country Roads of Quebec
Country Roads of Oregon
Country Roads of Washington

All books are $9.95 at bookstores.
Or order directly from the publisher (add $3.00
shipping & handling for direct orders):

Country Roads Press
P.O. Box 286
Castine, Maine 04421
Toll-free phone number: **800-729-9179**